A Journey of Courage, Vision, and Success

HER PATH TO
Entrepreneurship

HANNA OLIVAS
ALONG WITH 23 INSPIRING AUTHORS

TABLE OF CONTENTS

INTRODUCTION

Welcome to *Her Path to Entrepreneurship*, a tribute to the fearless women who have dared to turn their dreams into reality. This book was born out of a desire to illuminate the many unique journeys women take to become successful entrepreneurs—journeys marked by ambition, resilience, innovation, and unwavering determination.

Within these pages, you'll discover deeply personal and profoundly powerful stories from women across different industries, backgrounds, and walks of life. Each narrative offers an unfiltered look at the triumphs and trials that come with forging one's own path in business. These are not stories of overnight success—they are stories of persistence, courage in the face of adversity, and the bold pursuit of purpose.

The women featured in this anthology have not only built businesses— they've built legacies. Their insights go beyond strategy and profit to encompass mindset, leadership, and the transformative power of self-belief. They've faced fears, shattered glass ceilings, and leaned into their values to redefine what success looks like on their own terms.

Whether you're an aspiring entrepreneur or a seasoned business woman, this book was created with you in mind. It is both a source of inspiration and a practical companion—a reminder that you are not alone on this journey. Let these stories guide you, uplift you, and remind you that your path, no matter how winding or unconventional, is worth walking.

May these pages encourage you to step forward with clarity, courage, and the conviction that your vision matters.

Welcome to the sisterhood of entrepreneurs. Your path starts here.

Hanna Olivas

Founder and CEO of SHE RISES STUDIOS

https://www.linkedin.com/company/she-rises-studios/
https://www.facebook.com/sherisesstudios
https://www.instagram.com/sherisesstudios_llc/
www.SheRisesStudios.com

Author, Speaker, and Founder. Hanna was born and raised in Las Vegas, Nevada, and has paved her way to becoming one of the most influential women of 2022. Hanna is the co-founder of She Rises Studios and the founder of the Brave & Beautiful Blood Cancer Foundation. Her journey started in 2017 when she was first diagnosed with Multiple Myeloma, an incurable blood cancer. Now more than ever, her focus is to empower other women to become leaders because The Future is Female. She is currently traveling and speaking publicly to women to educate them on entrepreneurship, leadership, and owning the female power within.

A Journey of Strength, Opportunity, and Resilience

By Hanna Olivas

There's something uniquely powerful about being a woman entrepreneur. It's more than just building businesses or turning ideas into reality. It's about stepping into a role that not only demands courage but also an unwavering belief in yourself, even when the world around you isn't quite ready for what you're about to bring to the table. My journey as an entrepreneur has been filled with incredible highs, transformative opportunities, and yes, more than its fair share of challenges. But through it all, I've learned one thing: "When a woman believes in her own vision, there's nothing she can't accomplish."

Being an entrepreneur is a path I wouldn't trade for anything. It's full of possibilities, innovation, and, most of all, freedom. The freedom to create, to lead, and to make a difference in ways that resonate with who you are at your core. "Entrepreneurship is not just a career—it's a calling." It's a path that requires heart, vision, and tenacity. For me, it's been a path that's allowed me to live fully in my purpose, to build businesses that align with my passion, and to lift other women along the way.

But, of course, the road to entrepreneurship is not without its bumps. In fact, if I'm being honest, there have been many days when the obstacles felt overwhelming. As women, we often face barriers that our male counterparts don't. We're questioned more, doubted more, and, too often, underestimated. "Every woman entrepreneur knows the feeling of walking into a room where no one expects her to succeed—and the power of proving them wrong."

When I first started on this journey, I had big dreams. I could see the possibilities ahead of me, the potential to build something meaningful, something impactful. But I quickly realized that having a vision is only part of the equation. Execution requires grit, determination, and a whole lot of resilience. There were moments when I felt like I wasn't taken seriously, when people saw me as "just another woman" trying to start a business. And to be real with you, that hurt. It made me question whether I had what it took to make it.

But here's what I know now: "Doubt is just fuel for your fire." Every time someone questioned my capabilities, every time I faced a door that wouldn't open, I used it as motivation to push harder, to rise above, and to show that I was more than capable. Because here's the truth: "The biggest breakthroughs often come right after your biggest challenges." I lived that truth, and it's a lesson I carry with me every day.

Entrepreneurship has opened up opportunities I never could have imagined. It has given me the chance to meet incredible people, to collaborate with inspiring women, and to create businesses that are aligned with my deepest values. "As women entrepreneurs, we don't just create businesses—we create movements, we build legacies." Every business I've built has been about more than just profit. It's been about impact. It's been about giving back to my community, empowering women, and leaving a lasting mark on the world.

One of the most amazing things about being an entrepreneur is the ability to shape your own path. There's a freedom in knowing that you are in control of your destiny, that you get to decide how far you go and how big you dream. "As an entrepreneur, you hold the pen to your story—write it boldly." This freedom has allowed me to live a life that aligns with my values, to create a balance between my professional life and my family, and to design a life that brings me joy and fulfillment.

But with that freedom also comes responsibility. As women entrepreneurs, we often wear many hats. We are not only the CEO of our businesses but also the CEO of our homes, our families, and sometimes even our communities. Balancing all of these roles can be incredibly challenging, and there are days when it feels like there just aren't enough hours in the day to get everything done. "The struggle of balance is real, but it's also what makes us stronger."

There have been times when I've felt overwhelmed by the sheer weight of my responsibilities—times when I've questioned whether I could keep all the plates spinning. But I've learned to give myself grace. "You can't pour from an empty cup—take care of yourself first." It's a lesson that has been hard-earned for me. I used to think that if I wasn't always "on," always giving 110%, that I was failing. But I've come to understand that rest is not a luxury—it's a necessity. And taking time for yourself is one of the most important things you can do as an entrepreneur.

Another obstacle that we women entrepreneurs face is the pressure to prove ourselves in a world that still sometimes undervalues women's leadership. I've walked into meetings where my ideas were dismissed or talked over. I've faced moments where I was doubted simply because I'm a woman. But here's what I've learned: "Don't wait for validation from others—validate yourself." We don't need anyone else's permission to succeed. We don't need to ask for a seat at the table—we can build our own tables. And when we do, we create space for other women to sit with us.

One of the most powerful things about being a woman entrepreneur is the ability to break barriers, not just for yourself, but for the women who will come after you. I am passionate about creating opportunities for other women, about lifting as I climb, because I know how hard it can be to navigate this path. "When we rise, we bring others with us—that's the power of women in business." I want to be part of a legacy that makes the journey easier for the next generation of women entrepreneurs. I want them to see that it's possible, that they can dream big, and that they have the strength to turn those dreams into reality.

There have been moments along the way that have brought me to my knees. Moments when I wasn't sure I could keep going. But those are the moments that have shaped me the most. They've taught me that entrepreneurship isn't about never failing—it's about how you rise after the fall. "Every setback is a setup for a comeback." And trust me, there will be setbacks. But those setbacks are what make the success even sweeter.

One of the mantras I live by is "Stay focused on the vision, but flexible with the journey." There are so many twists and turns on the entrepreneurial path, and things rarely go exactly as planned. But that's okay. Success isn't about everything going perfectly; it's about being able to adapt, to pivot, and to keep moving forward, even when things don't go the way you thought they would.

Entrepreneurship has also taught me the power of perseverance. There have been days when I wanted to quit, when the obstacles felt too big, and the road too long. But something inside me always pushes me to keep going. "Your 'why' will always be stronger than your 'how.'" When you are deeply connected to why you're doing what you're doing—whether it's to build a better future for your family, to create something meaningful in the world, or to live a life of purpose—that's what will carry you through the toughest days.

I've also learned that one of the greatest gifts of entrepreneurship is the opportunity to grow—not just professionally, but personally. "Entrepreneurship is the ultimate personal development journey." It challenges you to face your fears, to push past your limits, and to become the best version of yourself. It forces you to grow in ways you never thought possible. And in that growth, you discover strengths you didn't know you had. You become more resilient, more courageous, and more confident in who you are and what you're capable of.

One of the challenges that I've faced on this journey is finding a community of support. Entrepreneurship can feel isolating at times, especially when you're navigating uncharted territory. But what I've learned is that "you don't have to do it alone—find your tribe." Surround yourself with people who believe in you, who will lift you up when you're feeling down, and who will celebrate your wins with you. There is power in community, and as women entrepreneurs, we thrive when we support one another.

One of the greatest joys of being an entrepreneur is watching something you've built grow and flourish. There's nothing quite like seeing an idea that started as a spark in your mind turn into something tangible, something real. It's the fulfillment of knowing that you created something from nothing, that you brought your vision to life. "There is no greater feeling than seeing your dreams take flight."

But along with that joy comes responsibility. As entrepreneurs, we have a responsibility not just to ourselves, but to the people we serve, to the communities we impact, and to the world around us. "Entrepreneurship isn't just about profit—it's about purpose." It's about using your business as a force for good, about making a difference in the lives of others, and about creating something that leaves a positive mark on the world.

As I reflect on my journey as an entrepreneur, I am filled with gratitude. Gratitude for the opportunities I've been given, for the lessons I've learned, and for the challenges that have shaped me. "Every obstacle is a stepping stone on the path to greatness." And while the journey hasn't always been easy, it has been worth it. Every challenge has made me stronger, every setback has made me wiser, and every success has reminded me of why I started in the first place.

To every woman reading this, I want you to know that your journey as an entrepreneur is worth it. There will be challenges, yes, but there will also be moments of pure joy, triumph, and fulfillment. "Success isn't just measured by the milestones you reach, but by the resilience, courage, and passion you carry along the way."

You are capable of incredible things. You are strong enough to overcome the obstacles, smart enough to navigate the unknown, and brave enough to pursue your dreams, even when the world tells you it's impossible. "The greatest power a woman has is the belief in her own potential, and once you embrace that, there's no limit to what you can achieve."

As you walk this path, remember to stay true to yourself. Stay connected to your purpose and grounded in your values. Surround yourself with people who lift you up, and don't be afraid to shine your light. The world needs more women entrepreneurs—women who lead with heart, who inspire change, and who uplift others as they rise.

Your journey is uniquely yours, and the beauty of entrepreneurship is that it allows you to create your own story. So go ahead—dream big, work hard, and trust that you are exactly where you are meant to be.

"She believed in her vision, trusted the journey, and became unstoppable."

And that, my beautiful sisters, is the essence of being a woman entrepreneur. You glow, you rise, and you thrive—despite the obstacles, because of the opportunities, and through the power of your belief in yourself.

Toni Thomas Durden

Personal Development Coach and Founder of Result Driven Life Inc.

https://www.facebook.com/toni.durden
https://www.instagram.com/toni_thomas_durden/
www.lifeinthejetstream.com

Toni is a successful entrepreneur, real estate investor, who has mastered the art of Airbnb hosting all while living a debt-free lifestyle. As a two-time best selling author, her impactful works, including "Life in the Jetstream" and collaboration with Jack Canfield, Chicken Soup for the Soul, in "The Road to Success Vol. 2," she inspired countless readers to pursue their dreams. A certified personal development success coach, Toni is dedicated to empowering others on their journeys to success. With over 30 years of a loving marriage to her husband, Rob, and as a proud mother of two sons, Austin and Kieran, she embodies the essence of resilience and purpose. Through her philanthropic endeavors, Toni continues to make a meaningful difference in the lives of those around her, proving that success is not just about personal achievement, but also about uplifting others along the way.

Create a Life and Legacy You Love!

By Toni Thomas Durden

A man without a vision will perish.

Over a decade ago, I created a company named Result Driven Life. I'd spent ages collaborating with coaches across every facet of my life. The company name was inspired by my goal of delivering visible results to my coaching clients. I had to reflect on my own life to identify where I had achieved the most effective outcomes. It's all about seeing things from a different perspective. Let me share a bit about myself and some life experiences that led to those results.

My bio reads, "Toni is a successful entrepreneur and real estate investor who has mastered the art of Airbnb hosting while living a debt-free lifestyle. As a two-time best-selling author, her impactful works include *Life in the Jetstream* and a collaboration with Jack Canfield, author of *Chicken Soup for the Soul*. In her book *The Road to Success Vol. 2*, Toni inspired countless readers to pursue their dreams. A certified personal development coach, she is dedicated to empowering others on their journeys to success. Toni has been married for 30 years to her husband, Rob. Through her philanthropic endeavors, Toni continues to make a meaningful difference in the lives of those around her.

"Behind Toni's remarkable success story lies a journey marked by profound challenges. As she forged her path, she faced unimaginable storms. These include the harrowing experiences of sexual abuse, bullying, substance abuse, violence, being shot, and raped. The trauma extended to the heartbreaking realities of dealing with the murder of her ex-boyfriend and the devastating impact of her father's suicide. The suicide occurred in the presence of her children. Despite these overwhelming obstacles, Toni demonstrated incredible strength navigating through financial ruin. Later, she achieved financial success, only to endure financial loss again to the tune of nearly a quarter of a million dollars. Recently, she confronted her health issues with six surgeries for skin cancer within a single year. Toni has not only survived, but thrived. She continues to use her life's experiences to inspire others and prove that resilience can lead to transformation, healing, and a deeper faith."

Despite facing numerous challenges, I have successfully maintained a 30-year marriage, emerging from a broken home. I have achieved financial independence, having been born into poverty. Through overcoming trauma, I have come to understand that adversity can be transformed into a profound gift, provided one does not succumb to victimhood.

Life is an intricate tapestry woven with moments of joy, sorrow, triumph, and tragedy. One of the most profound lessons I've learned is the concept of living the dash. I shared this in my first book, *Life in the Jetstream*. It is life-altering if you truly reflect on why you are here and what you want your life to stand for.

What does living the dash mean? The dash represents the time between our birth and death, encapsulated on your tombstones as the date of birth, the dash itself, and the date of our passing. The simple line signifies our entire existence—our experiences, choices, and the imprint we leave behind. It is our legacy. The truth is, we all have one, whether we consciously choose to shape it or not. I encourage you to be intentional about how you want your dash to look. What do you want to be remembered for? What mark do you want to leave on the world?

So how do we build a legacy worth remembering? Here are a few guiding principles that have helped shape mine:

1. **Embrace your story:** Every experience, good or bad, contributes to who you are. Own your story as a source of strength. Your struggles can inspire others and provide a sense of hope. Your story becomes someone else's survival guide.

2. **Be intentional:** Think about the impact you want to have on the world. Set clear intentions for your actions and strive to align your daily choices with your values and goals.

3. **Cultivate gratitude:** Acknowledge the lessons, learn from hardships, and find gratitude, even in the darkest moments. This mindset can transform your perspective and fuel your resilience.

4. **Serve others:** By giving back to the community, you not only help others, but you also enrich your own life. Acts of kindness create ripples that extend far beyond your immediate environment.

5. **Connection:** Build relationships with those around you. Support systems are crucial during tough times. Surround yourself with people who uplift and challenge you to grow.

6. **Pursue growth:** Never stop learning, whether through formal education, personal development, or life experiences. The best return on investment you'll ever achieve is investing in YOU. Growth is a lifelong journey.

7. **Live authentically:** Be true to yourself. Embrace your uniqueness and express it boldly. Authenticity fosters connection and inspires others to do the same.

8. **Joy:** Seek out what brings you happiness and make time for it. Joy is a powerful antidote to adversity and can provide the strength needed to face challenges.

9. **Know what you believe:** Faith, the size of a tiny mustard seed, is powerful. If you don't believe in something, you will fall for anything. God has been my rock and my foundation.

When discovering your legacy, ask yourself these questions: What will people remember about you? Did you love unconditionally, show generosity, and act with kindness? Were you joyful and adventurous, nurturing and charitable? If you have children, did you create an inheritance for them? Did you teach the younger generation a valuable skill and use your knowledge to help others? Have you contributed to making the world a better place? What impact did you make? Can you say that you ran your race well, without regret? When you reach the end of your life, will you be proud of what you accomplished?

Are you living life by default or by design? Can you honestly say you are creating the life you LOVE? YOU are 100% responsible for your choices. Ninety-seven percent of the population is dead or dead broke by the age of 65, with less than $2,000 in their bank account. When you realize this, you understand that something has to change. YOU MUST BE THE CHANGE!

My mentor shared something that made a huge impact on me. The definition of an excuse is a well-planned lie. She also said to weigh your ego with your bank account and see which weighs more. Well, that's a wake-up call! To build the life that you want, pride cannot get in the way. Pride will keep you broke.

Many of us were born in poverty and experienced childhood trauma. We had dysfunctional homes and absentee parents. We were surrounded by chaos, abuse, health issues, and other factors that made us feel unworthy to succeed. It allows us to make excuses as to why nothing works out for us. Sound familiar?

I have good news! There is a process to overcome this mindset. First, it comes with making a decision to not live a mediocre life—to stand up and do something GREAT with your life, despite your background. Most adults walking around feeling defeated are viewing life through the unhealed trauma of their past. We are knocked down by unmet expectations and are surrounded by fear of failure, the unknown, and judgment. We struggle with imposter syndrome, hiding behind lies, being a fraud, and not being good enough. One of the greatest secrets to success is to help others succeed. This is the secret to being UNUSUALLY SUCCESSFUL in ALL areas of your life!

Becoming an entrepreneur isn't easy. It's a daily challenge. Many people will tell you that you can't do it. Most people are speaking from their own insecurities, so don't let them determine what you can and can't do. I failed more times than I care to remember. It takes being passionate, tenacious, and persistent. It's having that NEVER GIVE UP attitude. It's being clear about what you want. Nothing becomes dynamic unless it's specific. Let me show you the difference. "I want to make a lot of money, to live my dream life, and to do what I want." Or "I want to make seven figures this year, build a thriving business with a minimum of 50 new clients, buy 2 more houses as an investment, and give away 15% of my income to those in need." Do you see the difference? You can measure and create goals for the second option.

You must know WHY you want to start a business. This is the key to staying focused and on course. What will motivate you enough to get up every day and focus on achieving your vision? Being an entrepreneur creates freedom, and I am ALL about freedom. Freedom to go where I want to go, do what I want to do, and live a life of financial independence that allows me to make those choices. I BELIEVE I can make a difference in the lives of the underdogs, the downtrodden, the poverty-stricken, and the abused. Having faith in Jesus allows people to be FREE from bondage and strongholds. I imprisoned myself with limiting beliefs about what I understood. Sometimes, it takes unlearning bad habits and faulty thinking to find what we truly believe in. I realized I was putting myself in a box. Actually, there was NO box.

The greatest tragedy in life is NOT death. It is not living the life that you've always dreamed of and settling for an unfulfilled life. It's having regrets about what you didn't do. The five regrets of dying are: I wish I had not worked so hard. I wish I had stayed in touch with friends. I wish I had let myself be happier. I wish I had the courage to show my feelings and live a life that is true to me instead of what others expected of me.

I began my search for a coach when I needed money, so I had a "business coach." I had no idea how my life would change so drastically. That business coach was in reality a personal development coach. This is the reason I have chosen to follow in her footsteps. Yes, she taught me about finances and how to make money, but I learned much more about myself along the way. Many times, we have no idea what type of guidance we actually need. However, I do know that if you don't deal with your past, your expectations, and your beliefs, you are doomed to repeat them. Being a business owner requires being intentional with what you do. It also requires being committed to a long-term vision that you want to see come to fruition. This means limiting your distractions, such as wasting time, scrolling social media, and hanging around people who consume your energy. I was fortunate to find the coaches I needed. I spent thousands of dollars to learn, heal, grow, be accountable, and be teachable. I learned a major lesson I'll never forget. If you can't find a specific coach or mentor, you need to STEP UP and BE ONE!

Money is a seed. What you plant, grows. If you eat all of your seed (which means spend it all), there's nothing left to plant to bring a harvest. We will have seasons of feasting and seasons of famine. Learn how to put away money for a rainy day. Be a good steward of all you are trusted with. If you are faithful with a little, you'll be a ruler of much. The more diligent you are, the more blessings will come your way. You have to check your motives and what you believe about money. When I initially started, I was desperate to make money. I had just lost everything financially. My mindset was wrong. I was coming from a place of a lack of understanding of how to use money as a tool.

In addition, I had to "get over" myself. We often focus on what we can't do versus what we can do. I started removing the layers of masks I was wearing so I could feel validated and appreciated. I had to face my fears of not being good enough. I realized that I had to change my surroundings. Your environment determines what level of success you'll have. For me, that meant changing friendships and finding people who had what I wanted so I could learn from them. You are the average of the five people you spend time with. Sometimes this means you must reverse-engineer your life. Start with what you want to achieve and break it down to smaller goals. Just remember, none of this will matter unless you know your WHY!

I want to encourage you to heal from your past. I want to challenge you to go after your dreams. I want to inspire you to Create the Life and Legacy you are proud of. I believe in YOU! This is your permission slip for you to grasp that you deserve all life has to offer. I am giving you a VIP ALL ACCESS Pass. The choice is yours. NOW. You are worthy, you are unique and wonderfully made, and YOU can make a difference. YOU ARE ENOUGH! You're not alone!

Here's where you begin!

Self-evaluation: Where are you now?

Write down what you want to achieve this year.

Start the process of healing!

Find an accountability partner!

Stop the excuses!

Discover your WHY.

Learn to LOVE yourself! HOW can we possibly love others enough to genuinely help them if we don't love ourselves?

Have integrity. Be your word! Be trustworthy and honorable.

There's POWER in words. Speak life over yourself and others!

The simplicity of success is right here. It's all about the journey of going from your head, which is selfish, to a heart filled with selflessness. All you need is to learn the way there. We are all born selfish. Circumstances and environment create negative self-talk and limitations. We must decide to change the way we navigate this path. Our growth is an inside job. Look at the words in the columns below. A great question to ask yourself is: What comes to mind with each word? Are you certain that what you believe is true? This is life's longest journey. Re-frame these concepts in your mind:

Head – Selfish	Heart - Selfless
Doubt	Faith
Fear	Love
Anger	Gratitude
Shame	Peace
Anxiety	Joy
Guilt	Humility
Judgment	Integrity
Hostility	Patience
Depression	Kindness
Lust	Sacrifice
Condemnation	Generosity
Competition	Present
Bitterness	Self-control

I'm blessed and beyond grateful for all that I've encountered in my life. It has helped me overcome obstacles that I never dreamed I'd conquer. My faith was built in a way that I truly have compassion for people suffering from multiple challenges in their lives. I have become the woman who always says, "What's possible?"

As the sun sets on this chapter, remember that every ending is just the beginning of something new. My hope and prayer for you is to Create a Life and Legacy you love. Don't wait for tomorrow. We are on borrowed time, and each moment is a gift. Choose you! Be courageous enough to follow your dreams and defy the odds. Design your life, craft it with intention, and shape your legacy into what you want it to be—a testament to your journey, your victories, your shared dreams, and the challenges you have overcome. Create a purpose in your life to inspire future generations with a heart full of hope and an unshakable faith. The world awaits your masterpiece!!!

Kira Ritchie

Go BIGGER Coach | dōTERRA Founder 2.0

https://www.instagram.com/gobiggermovement
https://www.thecreationplace.co/

Kira is a faith-driven entrepreneur, speaker, and legacy builder who helps women rise into their God-given purpose—especially when life feels like it's falling apart. After walking through one of the most painful divorces imaginable, Kira faced the impossible: becoming the sole provider for her children with no roadmap and no guarantees. Through surrender, vision, and grit, she became a U.S. Founder 2.0 with dōTERRA, leading one of the fastest-growing teams in North America. Kira's journey is a testament to what's possible when we choose to GO BIGGER—not by hustling harder, but by deeply aligning with divine timing, bold belief, and legacy leadership. She mentors others to rewrite their stories, claim their callings, and build businesses rooted in both purpose and provision. Kira is proof that the cave you fear to enter really does hold the treasure you seek.

The Bridge to Go Bigger: How Choosing Faith Over Fear Began a Legacy

By Kira Ritchie

My hands trembled as I gripped the edge of the counter, my heart racing twice the speed of the clock. Any minute now, the papers would be delivered to my husband—papers he wasn't expecting. Deep down, I knew this was the only way forward, but it didn't make it hurt any less.

As a God-fearing, family-focused woman, divorce was the "D" word—unspoken and unimagined. Watching my parents go through it was enough. Surely, it wouldn't be my story.

Yet, here I was: the weight of single motherhood and the role of financial provider looming over my head. I was raised by a single mom, and now I found myself walking in her shoes.

For the past eight years, I had been fortunate enough to stay home with my three beautiful children, tending to their ever-present physical, emotional, intellectual, and spiritual needs. I had worked with clients here and there, but it was never something I needed to do for income. Now, I found myself stepping into the dark.

Little did I know that the next three years of wading through the divorce process would be the darkest, heaviest, longest, most painful years of my life. Many have told me that they haven't heard of a divorce that was as cruel as mine.

The question that kept me on my toes was: How could I provide *well*, and still be present with the very thing that I value the very most:

My children?

Working 9–5 was NOT the answer for me. My soul *knew* it.

An opportunity emerged to become a second-generation United States Founder within the company, doTERRA—a holistic wellness company I had known and loved for years.

Only 200 spots.

Thousands upon thousands of people going for it.

First to get there wins.

What would it mean if I got a spot?

I would become a profit sharer in the next billion dollars worth of growth in the United States.

It would mean future financial freedom.

It would mean providing for my children in a way God knew I needed to.

It would mean freeing up my time to give back in all the ways my heart longed to.

And yet, the moment it was announced, I shut it down inside.

No way I could ever do that.

My leaders and team members buzzed with excitement at the news. They could already envision us there.

Not me.

I wanted to believe, but I just... *couldn't.*

Just the thought of it brought tears to my eyes, especially while thinking of the heart-wrenching divorce circumstances I found myself in.

A vision of sorts came to me one day as I was wrestling and looking deeper at the roots of my fears. It was as if I were standing at the edge of a cliff, facing a deep, rocky chasm, looking over at my leaders on the other side who had already made it to Founders.

One in particular, Heather, locked eyes with me. "Jump!! You can do it!"

Looking down into the chasm, my heart pounded with fear.

What if I don't make it?

I'll get really hurt—and possibly die.

It struck my core as I realized that this is how I saw the Founders' opportunity in front of me. I recognized how this deep-seated fear of failure—of disappointing others, and breaking my own heart—was holding me back.

I couldn't bear the thought of being hurt, disappointed, broken, and shattered, especially in light of the fact that my heart was already enduring the crushing weight of divorce. I couldn't be let down here, too. It felt safer to stay small than to risk the dream.

Our minds are hardwired to do everything possible to protect themselves from pain, be it physical or emotional.

So, of course, my mind was fiercely protecting me. And I knew that unless that shifted, I would never reach this dream.

Years of working with clients and imagery had taught me a thing or two about this.

I asked, "Is there another way to get across the chasm?"

I looked to the right, and there it was: a perfect, steady little bridge, leading to the other side of the chasm. Why hadn't anyone seen it? I ran to the bridge, and watched myself as I skipped across! This wasn't just about crossing a chasm, it was about choosing to *go bigger* in a way that felt aligned with grace.

It felt *effortless*.

It felt light.

It felt like *joy*, knowing that there was a better way!

And as I did so, I saw many others following behind me.

I noticed that they were carrying something.

We held in our hands large, smooth, round stones, flat and maybe five inches thick.

At first, I thought they might be symbolic of burdens, but upon questioning, I saw something different.

We got to the other side of the chasm. I watched as I laid the first stone, and subsequently, each person came and put stones on top of mine. I immediately recognized the scene from the movie *Moana* (I have kids, after all!). I was shown that the stones represented that I was here to leave a legacy for others to follow.

Wow... so this wasn't about a race.

Or competition.

It wasn't life or death.

I had been so consumed with wondering if there was "a spot" for me that I was missing the point.

Going into the journey, I limited myself to small, scarcity thinking by allowing myself to believe that other people needed this more than I did. I didn't think I could live with myself, knowing that I had "taken someone else's spot," someone else who had worked just as hard, and needed it more than I did.

The Cost of Playing Small

I had let this scarcity thought, disguised subconsciously as "consideration and compassion" for others, keep me from going bigger!

While sharing all these thoughts with my gifted mother, Karen Trifiletti (she has her Ph.D. in life coaching—highly recommend her!), she poured into me some wisdom that I will never forget:

"Kira, you can never take away from someone else's kingdom or glory... It's not possible."

Mic drop.

Truth bomb.

Whatever you want to call it, those words hit hard and sank deep into my heart. This freed me to *go bigger* without guilt.

It's exactly what I needed to hear to let go of my fear of competition— the fear that my success would somehow impair or hinder someone else's.

It was NOT true.

I chose to shed the belief.

I chose to surrender and RELAX into the timeline, and all the fears I had attached to it.

I found a quote that became my guiding force for the next three years. I wrote it in big black marker on the whiteboard in my home office:

"Until one is committed, there is hesitancy, the chance to draw back, always ineffectiveness.

Concerning all acts of initiative (and creation), there is one elementary truth, the ignorance of which kills countless ideas and splendid plans: that the moment one definitely commits oneself, then Providence moves too.

All sorts of things occur to help one that would never otherwise have occurred. A whole stream of events issues from the decision, raising in one's favor all manner of unforeseen incidents, meetings, and material assistance, which no man could have dreamed would have come his way.

Boldness has genius, power, and magic in it. Begin it now."

I invite you to read this. And read it again, and again...

If you understand *this concept alone,* it will change absolutely everything for you.

These words by W.H. Murray helped me realize—

I had to wholeheartedly commit to becoming a Founder.

I had to choose to go all in, 100%.

And choose again.

And again.

Choosing into my goal was something I thought I could do once, and be done!

But I realized that just as marriage is a choice—a choice to choose to love and trust every day—choosing to show up for our business is a choice. Every single day.

I visualized it in my mind. I felt the confetti falling on my hands. I saw myself hugging my business partners and beaming as we walked on the stage together. I embodied it as if it were already done. I wrote "I am Founder 2.0" on my mirror with soap, so I would see it every day! I wrote it into my signature Soul Story. I pictured my kids and me dancing around the kitchen, squealing with excitement, gratitude, and joy that I had finally hit Founders!

And then, I moved forward in faith.

No one imagined it would be a three-year journey—just as long as my divorce took.

I had one month left before the cutoff.

ONE MONTH.

There were still spots left.

Would I make it?

But I still had an enormous 400 points to go, out of the 1000 needed.

My mind raced back to the quote I had by then memorized:

"Until one is committed, there is hesitancy, the chance to draw back, always ineffectiveness."

Was I out, or was I in?

400 points in one month seemed impossible.

Most others had backed out on their belief that it was possible by this point.

Again, I had to decide.

"With God, all things are possible."

ALL things.

Did I really believe that?

I chose faith.

I chose to believe.

I committed myself.

"The moment one definitely commits oneself, then Providence moves too."

God showed up, big time! He gave me encouragement and support in the most unexpected, but most appreciated, ways. I could feel heaven cheering me on. Every time I wanted to quit, an undeniable witness would cross my path that this was still for me, IF I chose it.

Doors were opened, and last-minute miracles pulled through. Resources showed up. Not just for me, but for every single person who chose to believe!

"... all manner of unforeseen incidents, meetings, and material assistance, which no man could have dreamed would have come his way."

August 31st.

The final day. My heart raced as I cross-checked my math—it must have been a thousand times. 400 points in one month had felt impossible, yet here I was, just waiting for confirmation. When the phone rang, I could barely breathe.

"Congratulations!" the voice exclaimed on the other end. "You're now a Founder 2.0."

Relief swept over me, and tears rolled down my cheeks.

Not only did I make it, but I walked the stage, just as I had envisioned and written into my Soul Story, with 14 others from my team—rising together to become the fastest growing team in North America. We held hands and jumped up and down, beaming as the confetti danced around us. My kids and I squealed and danced around the kitchen–just as I had intentionally created in my mind.

No one had imagined it would take 3 years for those 200 spots to fill up.

And guess what? Only 167 out of 200 made it.

There were 33 spots left!

All that fear about "taking someone else's spot"—imagine if I had allowed it to govern me.

I wouldn't have made it. How many others on this journey had let that happen, I wondered?

Some of those were my team members whom I love dearly.

I learned to fully embrace the power of decision, coupled with vision.

A visionary friend of mine told me that the root of the word *decide* lies in the suffix "cide," which literally means "to kill." (Think of pesticides, herbicides.)

So when you decide, you are literally choosing to "kill" all other options! What is no longer an option for you? Write it down!

"Whatever you can do, or dream you can... BEGIN IT NOW."

You've *got* to GO BIGGER.

Few things will refine you as a person more than the process of starting and succeeding in your own business.

Why do I say that?

Because starting your own business means you get to face all your own stuff. It means listening to the little voice within you, calling you to rise higher, to go bigger, to do something greater, to bring YOUR unique, beautiful contributions to the world in a way that has never quite been done before.

It's one of the most vulnerable, soul-stretching journeys you can take.

It forces you to face your deepest dreams, fears, and inadequacies.

"Boldness has genius, power, and magic in it."

That magic is here for you.

So wherever you are in your entrepreneur journey, as my friend and colleague, Presidential Diamond Matt Hall says,

"Don't do it to see IF it works; do it UNTIL it works."

Will it work right away?

It's probably going to be a journey.

But AS you choose to commit and anchor it into your soul *as if it's already done*, doors will open. Providence will be working with you.

Nothing that you do in faith is in vain. It all works together for your good, for your learning, for God's glory.

You WILL be triggered, and you'll have moments when you want to throw in the towel.

But as you choose to face the blessing blockers with courage, then the whole world will open up to you.

"The cave you fear to enter holds the treasure you seek."

Will you dare to enter the cave? Face the unknown—the impossible, even?

So, my friend.

There are no coincidences. You're reading this chapter for a reason.

Just as every single author in this book has something meaningful that you can learn from, YOU have something meaningful that others are waiting for.

Time to unlock it.

Your *mess* can become your *message.*

Time to go BIGGER.

And if you need help having the courage to dream big, hold to your vision, and break through those blocks, feel free to reach out.

Here's to all the big, bold, audacious, wonderful ways you will shape the world.

Go rise, girl.

Tina Salmon

Founder and CEO of Coachanizer
Leadership & Life Coach, Burnout Expert, Licensed Psychotherapist

www.linkedin.com/in/tina-salmon
https://www.instagram.com/coachanizer/
https://www.thecoachanizer.com/

Tina Salmon is a Leadership & Life Coach, Burnout Expert, Licensed Psychotherapist, Speaker, Author, and CEO of Coachanizer, a business and wellness development company dedicated to helping high-achieving leaders sustain long-term success without sacrificing their health or happiness. With over 20 years of expertise in mental health, neuroscience, and business strategy, Tina has worked with entrepreneurs, executives, and business owners, equipping them with science-backed tools to optimize performance, manage stress, and create sustainable work-life integration. Tina partners with organizations to implement proven strategies that reduce burnout, retain top talent, and build resilient, high-performing teams. She is known for her direct, no-nonsense approach and her ability to bridge cutting-edge neuroscience with practical leadership solutions. Tina provides actionable insights that empower leaders to sustain their energy, sharpen their focus, and elevate both their personal and professional success.

Building a Life and Business Beyond Burnout

By Tina Salmon

I thought I had the path laid out: get my degrees, climb the corporate ladder, and hit the salary goals. It was stable and predictable, with limited risk.

There is beauty in life, we have our plans, and then there is the universal plan that serves the greater good.

I was born on the beautiful twin islands of Trinidad and Tobago to high school sweethearts. At just three months old, my father, only 23, was struck by lightning while fishing and passed away.

His sudden death caused me to unconsciously develop a belief that life was short. Growing up, I felt the constant urgency to accelerate everything because I felt like I was running out of time.

After migrating to the USA, I went through school, always striving to be the best, and by the age of 24, I had two master's degrees. Throughout my career, I became the top performer in every position. At 29, I was a director running four multi-million-dollar programs. I got married, bought a house, traveled the world, and made six figures, achieving the American dream until my body started giving out.

Fast-forward to 2020, at the height of the pandemic, I lost my father's only brother, contracted COVID-19, and faced an overwhelming workload in my 9-to-5 job. The juggling between work, maintaining my marriage, and simply staying afloat felt impossible. I was overwhelmed, overworked, and trapped in a cycle of stress and exhaustion.

I started getting frequent headaches, struggled with sleep, and couldn't shut off my thoughts. Even on date nights, my mind was consumed by work. My body began to send out warning signs: mental exhaustion, physical fatigue, and random electric shocks. Yet, like many high achievers, I believed that perseverance was the key to success, so I pushed through.

I did what most people do when overwhelmed: I tried to escape through distractions. I shopped online, booked spa days, indulged in wine tours, and downloaded another time management app. But none of these quick fixes worked.

Eventually, I went to my primary care doctor, who found nothing wrong. I saw a neurologist who, after less than 10 minutes, prescribed medication with harsh side effects.

Finally, I found a cardiologist who took the time to listen. After thorough conversations and testing, he suggested I might be experiencing burnout and encouraged me to address the root causes of my stress. Extensive research confirmed I was suffering from anxiety jolts, a condition where the body reacts to extreme stress.

The Light-Bulb Moment

I had been a therapist for 20 years, serving my clients at the highest levels, but I felt ashamed when I got burned out. I knew what I needed to do, like eating nutritious food, drinking more water, moving my body, getting quality sleep, and spending time with family, but that was far from what I was doing.

I was eating unhealthy food only when I felt hungry, stress-eating cakes, drinking water when I remembered, and barely moving. After all, I was tied to my desk, struggling to sleep, and wanting to be left alone because I was so tired.

This was a light-bulb moment. I realized I was not alone. Many high achievers know what they need to do to care for their bodies, but they are focused on getting the work done. Through my research, I found out that 50 percent of the workforce is burned out. I was on a mission to understand why, even though we know what we need to do to care for our bodies and manage stress, we so often neglect our needs in the pursuit of success.

After all, my nickname as a kid was "WHY," so why not get to the root cause and solve why we get burned out?

After thousands of hours and dollars doing this work, I discovered that three major factors cause burnout: societal pressures, workplace systems, and our relationship with time and money. While we cannot instantly change societal pressures or workplace systems, we can change our relationship with time and money.

What I found is that we all lived through major life events, such as the loss of a relative, that shaped our beliefs about life, especially around time and money. If those life events were traumatic, it exacerbates the impact because the brain is trying to keep us safe. If these major life events go unprocessed, they impact your ability to achieve your goals. They directly affect the thoughts, feelings, actions, and results you create in your life.

I had never processed the pain of my father's loss. I never truly grieved his passing, and because of that, I developed the belief that life was short and I was running out of time. Becoming a high achiever was how I coped. But it came at a cost, working nonstop and neglecting my most basic needs.

My Healing Journey

This light-bulb moment shifted my healing journey. I started to focus on my basic needs: eating healthy foods, drinking more water, exercising, spending time with loved ones, and seeking therapy to process the grief of losing my dad and uncle.

These actions helped restore my physical and mental health, but I quickly realized that life's stressors would always be present. What mattered most was how I responded to them, not how hard I tried to outrun them.

Reflecting on my past, I understood that losing my father and being raised to be a high achiever had shaped my beliefs about time and money. I worked relentlessly because I believed life was short, but that mindset led to burnout.

As I processed my experiences, I realized that my father lived his life fully, and I needed to do the same. I learned to cherish moments, take care of myself, and be present in my most important relationships.

I came to understand that while stress is inevitable, how we perceive and manage it truly defines our experience. The transformation was not just in my health, it was in how I led myself.

Out of this journey, I knew there needed to be a better way to live, one rooted in sustainability, not survival. I became a certified transformational mindset coach, and my curiosity about the brain led me to pursue certifications in applied neuroscience and neuro-linguistic programming.

Combining 20 years of experience in mental health and business, I started Coachanizer and developed the S.A.F.E. Methodology, a neuroscience-backed framework that helps high achievers keep their edge, optimize performance, and avoid burnout, so they can reach the next level of success without compromising their health or happiness. The methodology also helps organizations reduce burnout and retain top talent, boosting productivity and profits.

Test to Testimony

Coachanizer was born out of a gap in the industry. Like me, there are so many brilliant women working 70-plus hours a week consistently, unable to sleep, not eating well, skipping hydration, barely moving their bodies, and dreading time with loved ones. They are mentally and emotionally drained, physically exhausted, and simply burned out.

After opening Coachanizer, I found that many people needed the service but were unwilling to take the time to do the work. As high achievers, every minute counts, and we feel like we should always be working.

But here's the beautiful thing about the body: it will continue to give you signals. It's up to you to take action. Just like the check engine light in your car, if you ignore it, you will break down at the most unexpected time.

I had to make several pivots in my business from refining my ideal client to adjusting messaging, marketing, hiring, and systems. See, I never desired to have a business, but there was a greater plan in place.

Starting my business helped me heal major life events, like the loss of my dad, along with many other milestones throughout my life. Doing this work has made me pain-free, healthy, and the happiest version of myself. Burnout presented an opportunity to stop living by default and start living the life I deserve.

Building a Business Beyond Burnout

Building a business that feels good isn't just about financial success, it's about creating a life where your beliefs align with your results. Today, I no longer measure success by external markers alone. I measure it by how peaceful I feel, how much joy I experience, and how I show up authentically for myself, loved ones, and my clients.

There were days when I questioned whether I had the strength to continue. The financial risks, self-doubt, and fear of failure sometimes felt like too much. But then, I remembered my "why" and took another step forward, even when it felt hard.

As a high achiever, self-doubt is not just the occasional thought, it's the voice that gets louder with each new opportunity, especially when doing something new.

That voice that whispers: *Do you have enough experience? Are you qualified enough?* It reminds you of everything you haven't done yet, the certifications you don't have, and the experience you wish you had.

High achievers often fall victim to this cycle. We are wired for success and driven by the desire to constantly improve. This inner pressure to "do more" leads us to believe we're never quite enough.

For me, even with multiple degrees and 20 years of top-tier performance, when I started something new, I found myself asking, *What if I get this wrong?*

It's very easy to chase another certification, thinking it will fill the void and quiet the doubt. But no credential can do that. The internal voice is silenced only through the inner work, self-trust, confidence, and shifting your beliefs about time, money, and success.

S.A.F.E. Methodology: The Foundation of Success

The S.A.F.E. Methodology is not just about surviving stress, it's about building a life and business that allows you to fulfill your calling with ease.

S.A.F.E. stands for:

- Stabilize
- Align
- Fulfill
- Empower

Each of these pillars supports a Life First Business Model that prioritizes health and happiness while building a sustainable business.

This is not just about business strategy. It's about who you become in the process. Entrepreneurship is full of fear, self-doubt, and challenges, but it's also full of growth, clarity, and healing.

Stabilize the Mind and Body

The first pillar is to stabilize your mind and body.

Your body will always tell the truth. If you're feeling off, tired, or irritable, pay attention. You can't build anything sustainable if your health is falling apart.

Check in with a doctor to rule out anything medical. Oftentimes, we neglect to address medical issues that may contribute to the symptoms we're experiencing, keeping us trapped in a cycle of burnout. We need to make sure our physical health is in check before we take on the weight of building our business.

Action Step: Schedule your medical, dental, vision, gynecological, and other yearly checkups. Your health matters. When your body is well, your mind is clearer. You make better decisions and show up more powerfully in your life and business.

Align Your Vision

The second pillar is to align your vision for both your life and business.

As a business owner, you need a clear direction. Without alignment, you can get lost in the daily grind and lose sight of what matters. It's important to slow down to speed up; hustling harder won't get you there faster. When you gain clarity on your vision, you improve the quality of your actions and accelerate your success.

Action Step: Revisit your goals to ensure they align with your vision. Have you integrated your life and business goals, or are you sacrificing your peace for profits?

Fulfill the Plan

The third pillar is to fulfill the plan.

Once you've stabilized your body and aligned your vision, it's time to fulfill the plan. Break down your goals into specific, measurable, and realistic steps. Your plan should be flexible, allowing you to adapt to the ebbs and flows of life.

Fulfilling your plan is about quality over quantity. It is all about taking small, aligned, intentional, consistent actions that include prioritizing our health, relationships, and business success.

This is where we should focus most of our time. This is when we are faced with our greatest fears, which include self-doubt, fear of failure, and comparison, which may lead us to question if we even want to move forward. But it's also where the most growth happens.

Action Step: Set aside time weekly to review your progress, celebrate wins, reflect on your beliefs about time and money, and recalibrate your action plan.

Empower Yourself to Adapt

The final pillar is to empower yourself to adapt.

Change is inevitable. As a business owner, your success depends on how well you navigate uncertainty. Resisting change can lead to stress and burnout, while embracing adaptability keeps you strong and feeling in control.

Empowering yourself to adapt means embodying a growth mindset and recognizing that perceived challenges are opportunities for learning and setups for something greater. It requires self-trust, emotional resilience, and flexibility in both your life and business.

Action Step: When faced with challenges, ask, *What can I learn from this?* and adjust your strategy accordingly.

Building a business was never in my plan. But burnout pushed me toward something greater. This path is not easy, but it is worth it.

You don't need to have it all figured out to begin. You just need to show up, one decision at a time.

To the woman doubting herself: You are not alone.
To the one wondering if she is doing enough: You are.

And to the one ready to build something that honors her health, her values, and her future: Start now.

The business you are building is about more than profit, it's about peace and fulfilling your purpose with ease.

If you are feeling overwhelmed, take one small step today, book that health checkup, block time for rest, or simply breathe.

Building a successful business starts with building a healthy you.

If you are ready to lead your life and business on your own terms and avoid burnout, let's connect. I would love to guide you through the S.A.F.E. Methodology and support you in building a life and business that honors your energy, aligns with your values, and helps you achieve your financial goals.

You deserve a life and business that works for *you*.

Lovely LaGuerre

Founder and CEO of Pure Heavenly Hair, LLC

https://www.twitter.com/Heavenly_Pure
https://www.facebook.com/pureheavenlyhairboutique
https://www.instagram.com/pureheavenlyhair
https://pureheavenlyhair.com/
https://lovelysellsvegas.com/

ABOUT PURE HEAVENLY HAIR & BEAUTY

At Pure Heavenly Hair and Beauty our commitment to inclusivity and individuality is at the heart of everything we do. We celebrate all forms of beauty backgrounds, understanding that each person's journey is unique. Whether it's through our deeply moisturizing lip oils that enhance your natural glow or our go to wigs hair collections that bring life back to your locks, Pure Heavenly is here to honor and elevate your essence in every way. What truly makes us different is our belief in the power of connections with others. When you choose Pure Heavenly Hair and Beauty, you're choosing more than just a brand. You're embracing a lifestyle of conscious beauty, where every product is a ritual, every application a moment of self-care, and every result a testament to the heavenly within you. Come Unleash Your

Beauty From Within! Join us in our mission to redefine your beauty purely, naturally, and beautifully. Experience the heavenly touch of our products and discover what it means to truly elevate your essence with Pure Heavenly Hair and Beauty! Pure Beauty | Pure Confidence | Purely Heavenly You!

The Spark

By Lovely LaGuerre

I never saw myself as just a dreamer. I've always been a doer. But, like many women, I had to unlearn the habit of playing it small and start betting on myself. My journey into entrepreneurship wasn't born out of perfection; it was born out of a burning desire to create something meaningful. Something of mine.

I started with an idea scribbled in the back of my journal, fueled by passion, sleepless nights, and a whisper of a vision. What began as curiosity soon transformed into clarity. I wasn't just building a business, I was building a movement.

THE LEAP

Taking the leap wasn't easy. I walked away from comfort, predictability, and at times, the safety of a steady paycheck. I knew in my heart that I was meant for more. And with that belief came my boldest decision: to create a business that not only reflected who I was, but who I was becoming.

I faced doubt internally and externally. There were days I questioned everything. But what I learned quickly is that courage is not the absence of fear; it's taking the next step even when you're scared.

BUILDING BRICKS FROM BREAKDOWNS

The early days of my entrepreneurship were humbling. There were setbacks, missteps, and moments when I failed forward. But every stumble sharpened my strategy. I became resilient. I learned how to lead with heart and make decisions with wisdom. I discovered that leadership is less about having all the answers and more about being willing to learn, pivot, and grow.

From branding and funding to hiring and scaling, I wore every hat. And through the chaos, I found my rhythm. I realized that passion will get you started, but discipline and strategy will keep you going.

MY WHY

My "why" has always been about impact. I wanted to show other women that they, too, can own their power. That their voice, their ideas, their creativity, and their leadership matter. Entrepreneurship is not just about profit; it's about purpose.

I built my business to serve, to uplift, and to create opportunities. And as my brand grew, so did my mission. Today, I mentor other women, invest in communities, and speak boldly about my experiences, my worth, and the steps to take to thrive in business.

THE STRATEGY BEHIND THE SUCCESS

I learned that vision without strategy is just a wish. So I got it clear. I created systems, built a powerful brand story, leveraged digital platforms, and studied the market with intention. I didn't just hustle as I planned. I partnered wisely, aligned with the right mentors, and never stopped investing in myself.

One of my greatest lessons? Say no to what distracts you, so you can say yes to what defines you.

TO THE WOMAN READING THIS

If you're standing on the edge of your vision, wondering if you have what it takes, let me tell you: You do. Start being scared. Start small. Just start.

You don't have to know every step. You just need to trust that every move you make is building the path beneath your feet. You are not behind. You are becoming.

Your journey will look different from mine, and that's the beauty of it. Don't wait for permission. Write your own blueprint. Your story, your struggles, your strength, it all matters.

I am proof that you can go from overlooked to undeniable. From hesitant to unstoppable. This is your time. This is your path. Welcome to entrepreneurship, where your vision meets your victory.

GROWTH | SCALING | AND ELEVATION

As my business gained momentum, I realized success was never meant to be small. I had built the foundation, now it was time to scale. But with growth came new lessons: team building, automation, delegation, and managing expansion without compromising the soul of my brand.

Scaling wasn't about doing more, it was about doing things better. I invested in systems, strengthened my digital presence, and built and aligned myself with individuals who reflected my vision and values. I began creating structure around my brilliance because hustle might build it, but strategy sustains it.

I embraced my role not just as a founder, but as a CEO. I stopped wearing every hat and started building a company that could run without me. That's when true freedom began.

MENTORSHIP | LEGACY | AND GIVING BACK

One of my greatest joys has been mentoring other women who are just beginning their journeys. I've seen pieces of myself in every woman who was once unsure, scared, or underestimated, and I've made it my mission to guide, uplift, and open doors for them.

Legacy, to me, is more than revenue. It's what we leave behind long after the applause fades. That's why I share resources and networking with others where women can collaborate, share wisdom, and rise together. We are not competitors, we are collaborators.

When you build with the next generation in mind, you don't just build businesses, you build movements.

NAVIGATING CHALLENGES AS A WOMAN IN BUSINESS

Let's be real: being a woman in business is powerful, but it isn't always easy. I've walked into rooms where I was the only woman. The one they underestimated. But instead of shrinking, I chose to shine.

There were days I had to speak twice as loudly to be heard. At night, I worked harder just to be seen. But I transformed every doubt into drive. Every barrier into a breakthrough. I realized that I wasn't in those rooms by accident. I was there to change the conversation.

As women, we're not just rewriting the rules, we're creating new ones. Ones rooted in inclusion, authenticity, and unapologetic leadership.

REDEFINING SUCCESS ON MY OWN TERMS

Success used to mean external validation numbers, recognition, and awards. But now, it means alignment. It means peace, purpose, and the freedom to live life on my terms.

I no longer chase the spotlight. I focus on impact. I measure success by how many lives I've touched, how many women I've empowered, and how aligned I feel with my calling.

Being rich on purpose is the new wealth. And I wake up every day grateful that I chose this path, even when it was unreachable. Especially when it was hard.

THE GLOBAL CALL TO INSPIRING WOMEN EVERYWHERE

This story, this path, this purpose was never just for me. It's for every woman who dares to believe she can do more. Be more. Create more.

Whether you're in the beginning stages of your dream or deep into your journey, I want you to know: You are not alone. You are seen. You are capable. You are necessary.

The world needs your vision, your voice, your fire. Don't dim it. Let it burn so bright that others light their torches from your flame.

CONCLUSION:

A CALL TO ACTION

Her Path to Entrepreneurship is not a one-size-fits-all blueprint; it's a reminder that your path is powerful, no matter how messy or magical it looks.

To the woman reading this: Trust yourself. Bet on your vision. Build boldly and lead unapologetically.

Your dream is not too big. Your timing is not too late. Your story is not over; it's just beginning.

Welcome to the journey. Now go make your mark.

Valarie L. Harris

Founder and CEO of Varris Marketing
CMO & Coach

https://www.linkedin.com/in/varrismarketing
https://www.facebook.com/varrism
https://www.instagram.com/coachvalygrl1
https://www.VarrisMarketing.com
www.TimeFreedomFreak.com (Coming Soon)

Valarie L. Harris, known as Coach Valygrl, is the founder of Varris Marketing, where she helps entrepreneurs scale their businesses without sacrificing their time or sanity. As a certified business, branding, and marketing coach, Valarie empowers her clients to achieve time freedom through smart systems, automation, A.I., and strategic marketing. A firm believer in working smarter, not harder, she guides her clients to streamline their business operations, generate leads, and increase sales while maintaining balance in their personal lives. Valarie's mission is to help entrepreneurs leverage tools and systems that allow them to focus on what truly matters and avoid burnout. When she's not coaching, you'll find Valarie spending time with her retired sailor husband of 31 years, their three children, and her grandson. Living life to the fullest in the beautiful Pacific Northwest, Valarie is passionate about helping others achieve both business growth and personal freedom.

Fear, Faith, and Freedom ~ How I Built the Business of My Dreams

By Valarie L. Harris

"Entrepreneurship isn't just about making money; it's about creating a life on your own terms. The journey isn't easy, but neither is settling for less than you deserve."
— Valarie L. Harris

From a young age, I knew I was meant for something bigger than the 9-to-5 grind. Even as I built a successful 26.5-year career in corporate retail management, I was always searching for a way to create a life without limitations—one where I controlled my time, my income, and my future. The idea of working for someone else, following their rules, and being bound by schedules that didn't fit my life never sat well with me. I longed for freedom, and I was willing to explore every possible avenue to find it.

My first taste of entrepreneurship came in the summer of '88 while living in Okinawa, Japan. I was a nanny, and while I didn't see it as a business at the time, I now realize it was my introduction to the world of earning independently. I learned to negotiate pricing, budget my earnings, and reinvest in myself. That experience planted the seed, but my first real business came later—selling imitation cologne from the back of my trunk on the streets of Honolulu, Hawaii. It seemed like a brilliant idea until I learned the hard way that you need a peddler's license to operate legally. That was my first real lesson in business. Passion and drive are essential, but knowing the rules is just as important.

That setback pushed me into the corporate retail world, where I built a career that spanned over two decades. I excelled, earned promotions, and led teams, but in the back of my mind, I knew there had to be more. Throughout those years, I dabbled in different side hustles, desperately trying to find the one thing that would make me say, "This is it! This is what I was meant to do." I became a Mary Kay consultant, sold Kirby vacuum cleaners door-to-door, opened my own home daycare center, joined Avon, became an Herbalife consultant, and signed up for countless affiliate marketing and MLM companies. Each opportunity came with hope, excitement, and the belief that maybe this was the one. But time and time again, they weren't quite right—it was either the wrong time, the wrong fit, or just not aligned with my long-term vision.

By 2011, I was still working in retail, but my circumstances had changed. I was older, more exhausted, and facing a reality I couldn't ignore—I had a son with a brain injury and autism. The demanding, unpredictable life of corporate retail didn't align with the care he needed. Something had to change. That year, I took one last shot at building my own business and launched a personal assistant and errand service company. It started slow, barely making a dent financially, but then something unexpected happened. One of my clients asked if I could help her with her Facebook and Pinterest posts. I had no formal training in social media, but I gave it a shot. And you know what? I was good at it.

That client unknowingly planted the idea in my head—what if I could turn this into something bigger? I started researching, learning, and testing strategies. Social media marketing wasn't just a service; it was an industry with limitless potential. I pivoted my business, retaining the same name while transitioning into social media marketing management. Finally, I found something that aligned with my skills, passion, and vision for the future.

In February 2012, I officially launched I'll Get That for You Marketing. I was convinced that this time, success was inevitable. But reality had other plans. In my first year, I made $87. The second year, not much more. By 2014, I had to face the harsh reality—this wasn't working the way I had hoped.

Instead of giving up, I took a different approach. I stepped back, hired a business coach, rebranded, and restructured. That year off was the best decision I ever made because it allowed me to rebuild with clarity. In 2015, I relaunched it as Varris Marketing.

But let's be honest—it still didn't take off immediately. I made more than before, but something was still off. Through coaching, I was finally able to identify the problems. My pricing was too low. I wasn't outsourcing. My health was suffering from trying to do it all alone. And most importantly, I was still clinging to the security of my corporate retail job.

Then came 2016, the year that changed everything. My boss gave me an ultimatum: continue working or prioritize my son's care. That was the moment I knew it was time. I walked away from the stability of my corporate career and took the leap into full-time entrepreneurship.

Was I scared? Absolutely. But once I fully committed, everything started to shift. I learned how to price my services correctly, build a team, and manage my time efficiently. That year, my income tripled. And every year since, my business has grown beyond anything I could have imagined.

Looking back, I realize that the biggest obstacle in my journey wasn't the businesses I tried, the failures I faced, or even the financial struggle; it was fear. Fear of letting go of what was familiar. Fear of failing. Fear of stepping into the unknown. But once I conquered that fear, I stepped into the life I was always meant to have.

So, to every new, growing, or established entrepreneur reading this: **Keep going. Fail fast, learn faster, and never settle for less than the life you deserve.** The fear will always be there, but success comes to those who push through it. If I can do it, so can you.

Kaila Nike

Author

https://www.facebook.com/profile.php?id=61564802221645
https://www.instagram.com/kailanike.author/
https://www.kailanike.com/
https://www.tiktok.com/@kailanikeauthor

Born and raised in British Columbia, Kaila Nike is a dedicated mother raising two wonderful sons. While she earned a diploma in social work, writing has always been her true passion. Finding solace and expression in her words, Kaila focuses on crafting engaging narratives through poetry and fantasy.

Mind Over Matter

By Kaila Nike

Introduction

Fear and Desire are the basis of my chapter for the simple sake of simplifying things, as this is a chapter and not a book. But I want to share with you the struggles I've experienced on my journey in terms of mindset. I will provide some actionable steps that can be taken to pursue your dreams as an entrepreneur, then I will share with you my path and the life I've so gratefully built around it. Throughout this interactive chapter, note the songs I share with you that I personally have on my motivational playlist. The songs that I have selected are chosen intentionally because of the value they bring. This chapter might even show them in another light that you haven't seen them in before. I encourage you to take the time to fully immerse yourself in this chapter, do the activities I provide, and listen to the music with your soul while actively engaging with the words. This isn't a chapter that you're just going to read. It's a chapter that you're going to experience. So grab a notebook, your favourite pen, and whatever device you play your music on (I recommend Spotify or YouTube with lyrics so you can read long and follow the words). Let's dive in.

Fear

Fear was the biggest culprit. Fear had a hold on me that refused to let go, it clung like black tar on a hot day. Fear showed up in many different forms. Fear consistently urged me to stay invisible. If I'm invisible, then no one will know who I am. You can't dislike someone if you don't know they exist, right!? An invisible person can't be bullied, critiqued, shut down, made fun of, ignored, neglected, or even hurt.

I've always known deep down that I had a calling, a desire to be more than what I was. But every time I would attempt to take that leap of faith. Fear would stop me and pull me right back into my comfortable little zone. 'They won't like you,' fear would tell me. 'Who do you think you are? You have no value to give. You have an annoying personality, no one is going to resonate with you. You talk too much and you just say stupid things.' It was constant! And fear wasn't alone. Fear has many friends like anxiety, dread, apprehension, insecurity, panic, and so many more. And in my case, I imagine the reason they were so strong stemmed from a childhood of being bullied, abused, neglected, and cut down by so many people around me. There are some things even a mom can't comfort or fix. But those things, they stayed with me until adulthood. Fear was one of my best friends, well, more like my main frenemy.

**Write down the word 'fear' in the centre of the page and draw a circle around it. Then, branch off the things that fear and its friends tell you, just like in the example above. Once you have 5–10 samples written down, go ahead and play 'Zero' by Imagine Dragons. Remember that reading the lyrics while listening is important. If this exercise sparks an emotion in you, good. Bring the emotions up, let them be present. Listen to the song as many times as you need to. If you need to cry, cry. I cried. We're learning about the fear that has been holding you back. When you're done, come back and continue on with this chapter.

This song holds a special place in my heart, and believe it or not, it's my most-played song on this playlist. It's not motivational, though, is it? The reason I have it and listen to it so much is that it takes me back to a very real part of myself. The part that feels empty, the part that feels like I'm not good enough, the part that I believed to be my true self. It resonates with me, and if you're feeling stuck, like it doesn't seem to matter what you do, you just can't get ahead, then I hope it resonates with you as well. It's a place I never want to go back to, I need to feel these emotions to keep me from going back there because being stuck in that state was painful. It was only hurting me and keeping me from living the life I dreamed of.

Desire

Aside from fear, there were other emotions that stayed with me as well. Desire. Desire is kind. Desire motivates me and speaks kindly to me. 'You're meant to do this,' desire would say. 'There is only one unique you, you can offer the world what nobody else can, and you know what it is, it's in your heart. Never stop searching, never give up.' Desire is a light that, no matter how much I have been through, has always been by my side, some days shining brighter than others. Having these two 'friends' often felt like a battle of the wills. Desire was the angel on my shoulder while fear was the devil on the other, and they would compete to have their voice heard. Admittedly, a lot of times fear would win, and I would shut down and go back into my quiet little corner of the world. Then, once in a while, desire would come around and lift me back up again; sometimes, desire would even bring its friend, courage. And I would begin a new journey, a whole new chapter in my life being either starting a business, or volunteering, or beginning a new career. I'd always start out strong with the will to work my way to the top. But once I started getting to the top, I'd always self-sabotage because my dear friend, fear, would take the reins and the blocks would all come crumbling down, leaving me to once again start at point zero.

It was so incredibly frustrating. How could I have one voice telling me I can do this, I'm meant for more, all the while another voice is telling me the exact opposite, and both seemed equally strong, at differing points in my life. I felt like I was getting absolutely nowhere and that I was going to be a 'nobody' forever. No friends, no life, no real career, nobody. It was painful. And the worst part about it all is that my kids were watching. How can I teach them to be strong and believe they can do whatever they set their mind to if I couldn't even figure it out?

One day, I just had enough. It was time to begin creating more of the life I wanted. Not only in my dreams, but to make it a reality for myself and my kids as well. I let fear take the reins for far too long, and it was time for me to take things into my own hands. I had allowed desire to take the spotlight. But this time, desire didn't come alone. Desire brought a team load of friends: courage, motivation, ambition, passion, enthusiasm, vision, persistence, purpose, and many more. With my newfound strength, I spent years on my personal development. Yes, years, I had a ton of baggage to work through, and I want to share with you what I have learned, what has helped me become who I am today, and create the success that I've created. Let's hope it helps to fast-track your path to entrepreneurship.

Remember all those hurtful things we just wrote down about ourselves? Those have a name, and once we put a name to them, we have a newfound understanding, and we can begin to work through them. They're called limiting beliefs. They stem from the irrational sense of fear that you've adopted somewhere along your journey.

**We're going to go back to those words, and cross them out with only one line so you can still see what it says. Underneath those words, you're going to write the opposite of what it says. If you wrote 'I'm not good enough', cross it out and write 'I'm enough'; if you wrote 'they will make fun of me', write 'I am accepted.' And so on. Don't stop at just one truth; write down as many for each limiting belief as you can come up with. Because that's exactly what they are, beliefs that you have accepted somewhere along the road of time as your truth. But are they rational? Truly? Any negative thought or limiting belief can be shifted into something that serves you rather than harms you and your progress. The new beliefs that you just wrote down, replacing the limiting beliefs, are going to be your new thought pattern. Tell them to yourself every day: when you wake up, before you go to bed, when you look in the mirror, and eventually your subconscious will accept them as true. One, because they are true, and two, because your subconscious can't differentiate between what's real and what's imaginary and if you tell yourself something, you will begin to believe it as your truth (just like you did with the limiting beliefs) but now instead of the limiting beliefs, you're going to plant the seeds of empowering beliefs into your mind. Stay consistent, and they will take root and grow.

We're going to jump right into another song. 'Faith' by Fearless Motivation. Feel what it is you need to feel. Write down anything that comes up for you that you think can be worked through.

Fear continued

I always thought that fear was an obstacle, an unwanted evil entity solely designed to make you fail and keep you small. And while I thought fear was my enemy, I learned it's actually my friend; fear and all of its acquaintances are actually there to keep you safe. In its purest form, fear is a survival instinct, a vital mechanism that protects us from physical harm. The jolt of fear that stops us from walking into traffic, or the hesitation that prevents us from walking the back alleyway, are examples of this helpful fear. And sometimes, what we think is fear is actually our intuition telling us something is wrong. However, the trick lies in recognizing when fear is serving its protective purpose, and when it's morphing into something detrimental. Helpful fear is a signal based on a real and present danger. Unhelpful fear, or anxiety, is often based on perceived threats, past traumas, or irrational beliefs. Learning to distinguish between these two forms of fear is crucial. By understanding the roots of our fears, we can learn to manage them, allowing us to step outside our comfort zones and embrace the opportunities that lead to personal growth.

If you feel that fear is holding you back and you have the will to break free from fears that may have been created from past trauma, those types of fear may require professional help to work through. And I encourage that. There's no shame in that. I've sought professional help many times on my journey. It's not a weakness, it's a strength to recognize what isn't working and to seek help and support to work through and overcome whatever it is that's holding you back. I just have to say that the main thing that helped me overcome any obstacle is the power of knowledge. The more I learned, the more I leveled up. And I don't mean in an academic sense, I mean with my own personal growth. Knowledge has helped me to take risks, differentiate between rational and irrational fear and anxiety, and nearly overcome my anxiety disorder. Of course, I still get anxious; it's normal. But it's no longer consuming me.

**Now is the time to play 'Let It Go' by Idina Menzel. Yeah, that one.

Desire continued

You have that calling deep inside of you that wants to break free, demanding that you're meant for more. Well, here's the deal, it's not there by accident. That yearning, that insistent whisper in your soul, is a signal, a compass pointing you towards your unique potential. It's the echo of a purpose waiting to be realized, a contribution only you can offer. It's not a random thought, but a deep-seated drive, a part of you that refuses to be silenced. Ignoring it just denies a fundamental aspect of yourself, to live a life that isn't completely fulfilled. This calling can feel scary to follow (that's fear again), but it is in the pursuit of this calling that we experience the most personal growth. Ask yourself right now how long this calling has been inside of you begging to be released. Then ask yourself how bad you want it. If you want it bad enough, there's only one thing to do: it's simple, follow that feeling, even if it is hard.

**Whenever I think about purpose, the same song always jumps into my mind: 'You're Gonna Make It' by Dope Saint Jude. The lyrics describe how you're the only person in the world who can see the things you see. It's actually on my inspirational playlist and I admit I play it often, and have for years. I find it motivational because of the truth in the words. No one else in this world can see through your lens. You offer a unique perspective that deserves to be shared with the world.

Additional Actionable Steps

The five W's... and forget the H. Write down the answers to these questions. Be honest with yourself.

1. What. What is the desire that's tugging at your heart? What's your vision?
2. Why. What is your Why? What is at the very core of why you want this?
3. Who. Who will this serve? (Aside from yourself)
4. Where. Where can you do this? Online, in person, over the phone?
5. When. The time to get started is now.
6. How. Don't worry about the how. Once you're aligned with your desire, the how will take care of itself. The Universe will begin working for you, you'll start to see new opportunities arise, and that's when you take inspired action.

It always seemed like such a pipe dream to live the life I wanted. It seemed like no matter how hard I tried, I was never going to make it. And now, I'm sitting here writing, sharing my story with the world as a published author. I get to write for a living. I get to motivate and inspire while creating other worlds for people to escape into. This is my dream. It's not out of reach; all it takes is a shift in your mindset. If your mindset doesn't change, neither will your circumstances. If I can live my dream as a high-school dropout, full-time single mom, then you can, too. Check out my website by scanning this QR code, a small example of what's possible. I took the risk on myself, and I believed in myself. And I believe in you, too.

**Now that you've finished this chapter, queue the song 'Unstoppable' by The Score. The time for your next breakthrough is right now. What are you waiting for?

Additional Motivational songs:

'You're Gonna Know My Name' - Watt White, 'Lose Yourself' - Eminem, 'Show Yourself' - Idina Menzel, 'Woman' - Andreya Triana, 'The Champion' - Carrie Underwood, 'Never Give Up' - Sia, 'I'm Gonna Be Somebody' - Travis Tritt, 'Unstoppable' - Sia, 'Hero' - Fearless Motivation, 'Hall of Fame' - The Script, 'This Is Me' - Kesha, 'High Hopes' - Panic! At The Disco, 'Fight Song' - Rachel Platten, 'Roar' - Katy Perry, 'Warrior' - Fearless Soul, 'Google Me' - CLiQ.

Kimberly Laverdure

Kimberly Laverdure
Virtual Life Alchemist

https://www.linkedin.com/in/kimberly-laverdure-the-virtual-life-alchemist/
https://www.facebook.com/kimberly.smith72
https://www.instagram.com/kimberly_laverdure/
https://virtuallifealchemist.com
https://yourneighborhoodwitch.com

Kimberly Laverdure, The Virtual Life Alchemist, is a spiritual guide and business operations specialist who helps spiritually-minded, intuitive individuals align with their soul's purpose and create thriving, purpose-driven businesses. Combining personal transformation with practical business strategy, Kimberly empowers clients to heal limiting beliefs, trust their intuition, and design a life and business that reflects their deepest desires. Having faced her own challenges, Kimberly understands the importance of blending spiritual growth with actionable steps. Her holistic approach guides clients through defining their vision, setting boundaries, and taking inspired action. Whether deepening a personal journey or growing a soul-aligned business, Kimberly helps clients move from overwhelm to confidently stepping into their full potential. With her support, clients experience lasting transformation and confidently share their unique gifts with the world. Kimberly's work creates a balance between inner work and strategy, empowering clients to build businesses that nourish their soul and support their dreams.

From Systems to Soul: My Path to Alignment

By Kimberly Laverdure

How I Merged Strategy with Soul to Build a Business That Heals

For seventeen years, I've been helping entrepreneurs and business owners streamline their operations, automate systems, build and run their teams, and scale their businesses.

I've built workflows that turn chaotic businesses into well-oiled machines, ensuring everything runs smoothly. I run tech, event planning and coordination, and project management. I've been a Fractional COO and a manager.

I've helped them grow, organize, and function at a higher level. I helped them step into leadership and delegate so they can focus on their business and not be run by it.

But success isn't just about efficiency; it's about alignment. Over the years, I've realized that the most powerful businesses aren't just built on strategy; they're built on a foundation of purpose, intuition, and personal transformation.

My role has evolved over the years, but at its core, my mission has remained the same: helping business owners step into leadership, reclaim their time, and build something sustainable.

I thought I had the formula: strategy, efficiency, all-around support, automation. And for a long time, it worked.

But my journey into entrepreneurship wasn't just about strategy. It started from a place of necessity, resilience, and a deep desire for freedom.

A Business Born from Necessity

I didn't set out to become a full-time entrepreneur. My career began in the corporate and small business world, where I thrived in administrative roles, managing departments, and running other people's businesses.

But life had other plans. A major health crisis and an abusive relationship shattered the stability I had built, forcing me to a crossroads.

I needed to create a life on my terms.

At first, entrepreneurship wasn't a grand vision, it was survival. I started as a virtual assistant, leveraging my skills in organization and management to help other business owners. I built systems, managed projects, and handled back-end operations. The work was fulfilling, but I quickly realized something: I wasn't just supporting businesses, I was running them.

As I took on more responsibility, my business grew. I moved from being a VA to an Online Business Manager, then an Operations Director, helping companies streamline and expand. I began to understand the power of systems—not just in business, but in life. Structure creates freedom.

The Leap of Faith

The moment I knew I had to rely on my business full-time was both terrifying and exhilarating. I didn't leave my corporate and small business roles because I wanted to. I was forced to. When my health declined and I could no longer work in a traditional setting, I was left wondering: *Who am I if I can't work?*

Losing my children to parental alienation had already left me feeling stripped of my identity as a mom. Losing my ability to work felt like another devastating blow to my identity as a productive member of society.

The fear was suffocating. How would I provide for my children? How would I survive? But as soon as I started building my business, something happened. The fear didn't disappear, but for the first time, it wasn't in control.

I immersed myself in learning everything I could. Tutorials, platform courses, hands-on practice—I devoured it all. I trained myself on CRMs, SOPs, systems, platforms, and tech tools. I didn't wait until I was ready; I started before I felt ready, and that made all the difference.

Then, I got my first client. The one who truly needed what I could do. It was proof that not only could I make this work, but I could thrive.

Teaching myself everything from CRMs to SOPs, I dove into the online business world. I learned platforms, systems, and automation, determined to create a career that allowed me to work despite my health challenges.

And slowly, I built something sustainable. The work relieved my anxiety, fears, and depression. Even though it was completely new, I thrived.

In many ways, rebuilding my business became a way of rebuilding myself.

A Lesson in Resilience

Through every business I've built—whether it was a record shop, a VA business, or my spiritual guidance practice—I've learned invaluable lessons. Some were learned through trial and error, others through watching those around me.

One of the biggest takeaways? High-touch, white-glove service matters. From my father's business to my own, I learned that attention to detail and exceptional customer service separate businesses that thrive from those that struggle. Whether I was managing insurance submissions, handling logistics, or ensuring seamless event production, one thing remained true: clients remember how you make them feel.

I also learned that resilience and adaptability are non-negotiable. Nothing in business goes exactly as planned. I saw this firsthand when my record store closed, when I had to pivot after my health forced me out of traditional work, and every time a client's needs shifted unexpectedly. The ability to pivot, learn quickly, and remain open to new opportunities is what kept me going.

But resilience isn't just about business. It's about identity. Through every shift and reinvention, I kept coming back to the things that made me, *me*. And at the core of it all was writing.

A Story Reclaimed

My love for writing began at six years old. I always envisioned a career in storytelling, believing my words would shape my future. At the same time, my entrepreneurial spirit emerged. By 17, I was already starting side businesses, driven by curiosity, ambition, and a desire for independence.

But life took a different turn. Marrying young and starting a family put my writing dreams on the back burner. The demands of survival and an increasingly abusive relationship silenced the storyteller in me.

Silence became my safest refuge. The more my voice was stifled, the more my ability to express myself faded. For years, my words remained locked inside, buried under responsibilities and hardship.

Yet writing never truly left me. When I stepped into the online space, I found a way to rekindle that part of myself. Becoming the Editor-in-Chief of a magazine reawakened my love for words, even if I was shaping others' stories rather than my own.

When I transitioned into VA work, writing and copy editing became key parts of my skill set. I helped clients craft their messages, refine their branding, and elevate their content. Unknowingly, I had begun merging my writing with my business expertise. I had spent years helping others refine their words, but it was time to reclaim my own story.

Then came the moment that changed everything: I took a leap to join an amazing group of women to co-author my first published anthology. A bestselling book in the U.S. and internationally.

It wasn't just about being published. It was about reclaiming my voice. That book reignited my passion for storytelling, proving that my words mattered. And from that moment, writing was no longer just a skill—it was part of my purpose.

My writing process is an intuitive flow. It pours out of me. After years of silence, once I started writing again, it was like I couldn't stop.

Writing has always been a form of self-expression, processing, and healing. My blog, my copywriting, my client work; all of it ties back to storytelling. And that's what I've realized: writing is the bridge between my two worlds.

It helps me explain what I do and why it matters. It connects me to clients. And, most importantly, it's a tool for personal and business transformation.

Seeing my book published was emotional. I cried when it was released, I cried when we hit the bestseller list, I cried when I held my paperback for the first time. It's still new, having just been released in January 2025, but I know this is only the beginning (as I'm now writing this as another co-authored work).

Now, writing has become an essential part of my brand and my life. I use it in business—educating, inspiring, and connecting with my audience through blog posts, email newsletters, and social media.

My words are more than just content; they are a tool for transformation, not just for me but for those I serve.

Now, I'm preparing for my signature business book and my first fiction novel. Writing has become a driving force in my work. Whether through blogs, articles, poetry, journaling, or books, it's my artistry, my form of self-expression, my healing process.

A Business Beyond Systems

But still, I kept getting the nudge. That little voice that wouldn't stop saying there's more to what you're doing.

I didn't fully realize what was missing until I found myself behind the scenes at an Online Live event—a three-day immersive experience. I was hired to handle all the technical aspects: running the event's backend, ensuring smooth transitions, and putting out digital fires before they could even spark. This was my sweet spot. Or so I thought.

While I was deeply focused on the logistical side, something unexpected happened: I was profoundly impacted by the teachings. As I listened to the speakers, something stirred within me. Their words about purpose, alignment, and deeper meaning resonated in a way I hadn't expected. It was like the final piece of a puzzle clicking into place.

And just like that, the realization hit me. It was never just about systems. It was about the souls behind them. Helping people step fully into their purpose, not just their strategy.

I had spent years perfecting systems and structures, but business success isn't just about automation and efficiency. There's another side to the equation: healing, intuition, and spiritual growth.

I'd been a psychic, intuitive, and medium since I was a small child. I'd tried to build that business separately from my other one. But there was always that little voice saying, *"Bring them together. Do both."*

One of the greatest lessons in my entrepreneurial journey has been learning to listen to my intuition. It guides everything I do, but learning to trust it was the real challenge.

I remember early on, taking on clients when I knew something felt off. Maybe the energy was wrong, maybe they weren't aligned with my way of working, but I ignored my gut because I needed the money. Every time, it ended in frustration, scope creep, and exhaustion.

I started working with clients in a new way. One that blends business strategy with deep personal alignment. I began incorporating intuitive insights into my coaching sessions, guiding entrepreneurs to uncover hidden beliefs that were keeping them stuck. I encouraged them to align not just their workflows, but their energetic presence in their business.

I use my intuition to guide my work, receiving downloads, insights, and knowing when I'm on the right path with clients. I hold their vision and future planning, helping them not just build businesses but transform their lives.

And the moment I started listening—when I turned down a bad fit client even though I needed the money—an amazing opportunity always followed. Every. Single. Time.

Now, intuition is built into how I run my business. It's how I guide them, and myself, not just with systems and strategy, but by seeing who they are becoming and how they can step into that next level.

A Turning Point in My Own Business

As I went deeper into this work, I realized something huge: I wasn't just helping my clients scale their businesses; I was helping them heal.

Healing the fear of success. Healing the burnout that comes from over-hustling. Healing the belief that they have to "do it all" to be worthy of success.

But I didn't dive in headfirst. I gave myself permission to unfold—to explore this new direction without rushing it, to test how it felt, and to embrace the shift at a sustainable pace.

I began asking different questions. Instead of just focusing on what business owners needed to do to optimize their systems, I started asking:

- Where are they feeling blocked in their business?
- What personal patterns are affecting their ability to scale?
- How can they integrate healing and growth into their leadership?

I started working with clients in a new way. One that blends business strategy with deep personal alignment. I began incorporating intuitive insights into my coaching sessions, guiding entrepreneurs to uncover hidden beliefs that were keeping them stuck. I encouraged them to align not just their workflows, but their energetic presence in their business.

And the results? Remarkable.

It wasn't just about the systems anymore. It was about who they were becoming as they built their businesses.

And that, I knew, was the missing link.

I wasn't pivoting. I was integrating.

And in guiding others, I found myself healing alongside them. No longer do I allow my identity to be defined by what I can or cannot accomplish, but by who I am at my core. I've learned that I am the architect of my own life, capable of rising above limitations and stepping fully into my purpose.

A Bridge Between Two Worlds

Today, my work has evolved into something that is both deeply practical and deeply transformational. My writing is back in full force and used to inspire, teach, and entertain.

I still bring strategy, automation, and optimization to the table. Because those things matter. But now, I also bring an understanding of the human experience behind business success.

I help my clients not just build systems, but break through personal barriers that keep them from scaling. I guide them to align their spiritual growth with their business goals.

It's a slow, steady unfolding. One that continues to evolve. And while I don't have all the answers just yet, I know this: This is the work I was meant to do.

A New Way Forward

The next evolution of my work isn't just about business coaching and business management—it's about deep, transformational healing.

I envision leading private healing retreats where people come not only to rest but to deeply align with their purpose and create a vision for what's next. A weekend of deep healing, followed by tangible action steps for the business and life they want to build.

I envision a future where I help entrepreneurs step into their full potential. Not just as business owners, but as whole, aligned individuals.

I envision bringing other experts together to guide my clients in areas I don't.

And as my team continues to handle the business side, the systems and processes, I'll be stepping more fully into my highest purpose: guiding people to build not just businesses, but legacies.

This isn't just a business; it's a movement. One where entrepreneurship, healing, and purpose merge to create lasting change.

A Path to Alignment

If you're reading this, you might be standing at a crossroads, too. Maybe you've built a successful business, but something still feels misaligned. Maybe you're craving more meaning in your work. Maybe you've been feeling that nudge—the one that's asking you to step into something deeper, more purposeful, more fulfilling.

I want you to know: *That feeling is worth exploring.*

True business success isn't just about scaling up. It's about stepping fully into your purpose. And sometimes, that means integrating the parts of yourself that you've been holding back.

So, here's my invitation to you: *Trust the unfolding.*

Because when you align every part of yourself with your business— your strategy, your intuition, your soul?

That's when the real magic happens.

Kimberly Laverdure
VirtualLifeAlchemist.com
YourNeighborhoodWitch.com

Hannah Darby GMBPsP SMACCPH

Healing with Hannah
Therapist: Founder of Kintsugi Method with H.E.A.L approach

https://www.linkedin.com/in/hannahdarbyhealingwithhannah
https://www.facebook.com/hannahsdarby
https://www.instagram.com/healingwithhannahd/
https://www.accph.org.uk/united-kingdom/martley/therapists-and-coaches/hannah-darby
https://www.healingwithhannah.co.uk/

Hannah Darby GMBPsP SMACCPH is an award winning trauma therapist who helps guide individuals on their personal grief journey. Hannah's unique Kintsgui Method and H.E.A.L approach has been featured in the international magazines, She Wins and Becoming an Unstoppable Woman. Hannah is a General Member of the British Psychological Society, a Senior Member of Accredited Counsellors, Coaches, Psychotherapists and Hypnotherapists, a Reiki Master, a HeartHealing® practitioner, Masseuse and an International Bestselling Author. Hannah runs Healing with Hannah, a unique therapy practice based on her professional and personal wisdom guided by science and spirituality. Hannah guides people on their personal grief journeys with care and compassion. Hannah works with their mind, heart and body to help them find deep healing with soulful integration. Hannah resides in the British Countryside with her husband, four cats and two chihuahuas. Hannah loves heavy metal, horror movies and long country walks.

The unexpected path to entrepreneurship

By Hannah Darby GMBPsP SMACCPH

Running your own business takes strength, courage, and resilience. It's not a path for the faint-hearted; it is full of tears, yet also a lot of laughter. It's a labour of love. You have to be willing to go the extra distance and tackle what seems impossible at the time in order to chase your dreams. You have to take on all of the employee identities of a company at the same time—CEO, Finance, HR, Sales, Marketing, Advertising, Complaints, Communication, Design, Technical Support, PR Relations, Customer Service... Wearing all these different hats at the same time is one of the biggest challenges I have found on my pathway to becoming an entrepreneur.

I feel it is especially harder to build a business as a woman. We are expected to run the household, be mothers and wives looking after our family, and run our business all at the same time. It is especially more challenging when living with a disability as I do. I refused to let my disability stop me from achieving my dreams. If you want it bad enough and are willing to trade blood, sweat, and tears, then go ahead and chase your dreams. If you never try, you will never know!

It's funny, but I never really thought of myself as an entrepreneur until I signed up to take part in this project. I have just been boldly pursuing my dream, letting my heart lead and listening to the whispers of my soul. The path to entrepreneurship is winding and unexpected, yet worth every moment.

I'm the founder of Healing with Hannah, an award-winning therapy and coaching service with a specialty in grief. Using my signature Kintsugi Method with H.E.A.L approach. I guide you to—Heal your relational wounds of your heart, Express your anger and pain, Accept your new reality, and show you how to Learn to Live and Love again. I'm so thankful that I have had the support of my family who have backed me every step of the way. I'm also thankful to my mentors, as well as networking groups full of other women in business who have given me so much guidance along the way. I'm relatively new to this, having only been operating for just over a year. Most businesses fail in the first year, so I am happy to have made it past that hurdle!

I have created my own website (that's now been revamped by the pros), whilst continually studying to deliver the best possible therapy to my clients. I have decided on what direction to take my business. I have navigated personal visibility hurdles left over from decades of bullying by posting publicly on social media, taking part in live videos, and appearing in podcasts. Even writing books, which was a lifelong dream of mine, proudly becoming an international bestselling author, and even appearing in international magazines. I feel so lucky to have been able to fulfill a lifelong dream. I have loved my writing journey and advise you to embrace your fear, turning it into excitement, and follow your dreams.

The biggest barrier I personally have faced on my journey is myself. Ignoring the negative comments in my mind and overcoming visibility fears after decades of bullying has been hard! It's safe to say I am always my own worst critic—not listening to this critic is difficult. It takes strength and courage to put yourself out there and become the face of your business, with no one else to hide behind. But this has healed me in ways I never imagined. Showing me how confident I actually am, how my words bring inspiration to other women. Having lived my life, it just seems normal to me, but describing it to others and having them tell me my words have inspired them is one of the greatest gifts I have received in my entrepreneurial journey.

Why did I choose this path? Well, I have always known I'm here to help guide others. I'm empathic, compassionate, and a good listener. People have always opened up to me about the darkest moments in their life story after minutes of meeting me. I have the gift of a strong intuition, am great at reading people, and have a gift for reading energies. However, I did not want to go straight into therapy when I finished college, as I felt I needed more life experience.

Having been severely bullied all the way through my education, this left me with little self-worth and rock-bottom self-esteem. Even though I never showed the bullies on the outside how much they affected me, their words cut deep and left lasting emotional scars. Then, when I was thirteen, my father died of a heart attack in front of me on my grandmother's sofa as I was bringing him a cup of coffee. He wasn't the first death I experienced, nor was he the last, but it was definitely the one that changed me the most. I felt so alone, with no one to turn to; I just wanted to numb the pain and escape the reality of the daily bullying. So, I drowned my sorrow in alcohol, drugs, and self-harm. Grief never leaves us, it changes us forever.

I went on to study Psychology at A-level and degree level in an attempt to understand myself better, why I felt the way I did. I realised I was severely depressed and anxious. The only place I found any comfort was in the lyrics of the metal songs I listened to. I felt that if they could get through it and become rock stars, then I could get through it, too. I knew I had to have a break, I had the opportunity of travelling before university, so I grabbed it with both hands. So at only eighteen, I took myself off on my own on a gap year to New Zealand on a working visa. I learnt so much about myself during this time, that I was confident and I could make friends and people did like me! When I started my degree at university, the girls in my hall of residence named the kitchen after me, making a sign for the door—'Hannah's kitchen of love, come in and have a cup of tea'. This was one of the best gifts I could have ever asked for. It showed me my kindness was still strong and that I was valued.

After university, I graduated in the middle of the financial crash of 2008 and struggled to get a job. It got to the point I needed to earn so I had to take a job, any job. I ended up going between lots of different roles, getting an itch to move around every four years. I went from Kitchen Manager to Retail Assistant, from Front of House staff to Historic Property Guide. Then a life-changing car accident started to point me along the path of an entrepreneur. I broke my back, leaving me living a life in chronic pain. I wanted a change, so I retrained as a Dental Nurse. Quickly, I realised that this was a bad move, as so much of the time is spent bending over, not good for my back.

Unbelievably, another health crisis hit me. I developed ME/CFS after a bad viral infection. It took over a year of tests, appointments, scans, and trying different medications to finally get a diagnosis. There is no cure; the only thing that helps is learning to listen to your body and pace well, conserving energy as the precious resource it is. It is so much more than fatigue. It affects every aspect of your life, with a myriad of symptoms, including brain fog, which is so frustrating. Safe to say, this put an end to my career in Dentistry, which was not a bad thing at all. It had run its course for over eight years being a General Nurse, Specialist Implant Nurse, Radiography Nurse, and finally Compliance Manager.

However, I'm so pleased in a way as it put me onto this path I am on now. The path of an entrepreneur. It pushed me back onto my true soul path, and now my heart sings every day. We only get one life, so we must chase our dreams. It's funny how when one door closes, another opens. This is my unexpected path to entrepreneurship.

I knew I needed to work on myself more, so a friend recommended Reiki to me. I found it so transformational in helping me to truly be present in the moment, helping to quieten my racing mind. I became a Reiki Master, dedicating myself to learning and expanding. I still felt something was missing, this is where HeartHealing™ came in. This fabulous therapy focuses on healing trauma through the relationships surrounding an experience. I had tried conventional therapies, CBT and ACT, they never worked on me, but HeartHealing™

allowed me to be happy as myself for the first time in my life. As part of the training, they also give business support. So with their guidance, I started Healing with Hannah. I quickly won a business award for inspiring others. I knew that this was where I was meant to be. I can manage my disability so much better, resting when I need to and working around my symptoms has been hugely transformational.

The path to running a business and becoming an entrepreneur is tough, yet so rewarding. Running a therapeutic business, you are selling yourself, not just the modalities. Selling who you are, your thoughts and beliefs, your own personal healing journey. This is what makes me different from any other therapy practice: I lead with my heart and come from a place of true understanding of what it is like to live in grief. I have lived my whole life in grief, grief for lost loved ones, grief for lost parts of myself with accident and illness, and a collective grief of the environment. Living in the countryside all my life, I have seen the effects of the climate emergency firsthand and hear Mother Nature crying every day. This is why I specialise in grief, as grief has always been a part of my life. It is not something to be scared of, something to bring us down, but rather a testament to our love, devotion, and ability to care. It's a deeply personal journey, but one that does not need to be walked alone.

This was the beginning of Healing with Hannah. I have already impacted so many lives, and have a bank of beautiful testimonials, and this is only the beginning! I know I am here to make a difference.

So what have I learned that I can share with you along this path to entrepreneurship? You have to be brave and bold, make decisive decisions, and take fast action. You have to trust your instincts and go with your gut. You have to manage your time effectively and avoid procrastination. You have to let go of perfectionism; done is better than perfect. You have to let yourself be guided by others, there is no need to reinvent the wheel. You need to have a clear idea of what you want to achieve and trust with blind faith that the path will become clear once you start to walk it. You have to put yourself out there, network, and learn how to communicate what you do in a few words. You have to let go of fear, push yourself outside your comfort zone, and embrace the unknown. You have to plan for the unexpected. Let your passion drive you and be your authentic self. People like to buy from and work with real people, it doesn't matter if you don't have it all figured out. After all, business is an experiment. If it doesn't work, tweak it and try again, but never take the results personally. Ensure you make a space between yourself and your business. There are no failures or mistakes, just lessons to be learnt. So dust yourself off and try again. Everyone starts somewhere; after all, you never know until you try. What are you waiting for? Go on, give it a go and chase your dream.

Work out what your values are, the why behind your business, and your mission statement. Let this be your guide, and when it all seems too much, fall back on your why to give you courage and strength. Let your values be the pillars of your business and remember your bigger mission. My core business values are compassion, courage, and safety. I believe in a world where I can empower people to navigate grief, embrace their authentic selves, and find light even in their darkest moments. My why is that we live in a world where grief often feels isolating and unseen. I create a space where the invisible becomes visible, where pain is met with compassion, and where healing is not just possible but inevitable. Through my work, I help people reclaim their joy, honor their past without sorrow, and step into a future where they are free to live and love fully, knowing that even in the hardest moments, they are never alone. My mission is to guide others through their grief journey with empathy, strength, and a deep sense of safety—helping them heal, find peace, and move forward with love, free from guilt or shame. When it all gets overwhelming, I focus on my values, my why, and my mission to help give me the strength to carry on. Knowing that my business is bigger than me, not constricted by my limitations, and with courage and compassion, I can achieve the unachievable.

I did all my training, built my business, created a website, designed my logo, created my signature programme—the Kintsugi Method with H.E.A.L approach (which has been featured in international magazines), and secured my first clients, all while living with a debilitating disability. Yet this is part of my strength, my uniqueness, what makes me different, and the basis I feel for where a lot of my compassion lies. If you are struggling with health issues, do not let that stop you, you are so much more than just your disability, your diagnosis. It does not define who you are, who you can be, or what you can do. This can be your strength if you use it well, as it gives you a view of the world that many others cannot see. It gives you a unique advantage, enabling you to see life from a different point of view.

Whatever your idea, your business, your passion, go out there and start your own path to entrepreneurship, knowing that you are never alone and it is definitely worth fighting for. This is a community that, once you are a part of, you will never dream of walking any other path again.

Nikki Hillhouse

nikkihillhouse.com
Mindset and Therapeutic coach

https://www.linkedin.com/in/nikki-hillhouse-a6b25529b/
https://www.facebook.com/nikki.hillhouse.1
https://www.instagram.com/nikkihillhouse/
https://www.nikkihillhouse.com/

Nikki is an experienced Mind Detox Practitioner, Meditation Teacher, Well-being Coach, International Speaker, Wellness Retreat Facilitator, and Writer. With a rich background in holistic health and therapeutic techniques, she is dedicated to helping others unlock their full potential. Her mission is to empower others to overcome their greatest challenges, transcend fears, and step into a life of freedom, happiness, health, and fulfillment. With a great passion is to help clients reconnect with their intuition, heal past wounds, and embrace their worthiness. Through her holistic approach, Nikki guides individuals toward self-discovery, resilience, and personal transformation, inspiring them to create a life without limits. Nikki has transformed her life from chronic pain and struggle to radiant health and resilience. Her journey led her from adversity to the tranquil shores of Turkey, where she now hosts transformational wellness retreats and runs a thriving coaching business, guiding others toward empowerment, transformation, and lasting well-being.

Turn the Impossible Into Limitless Possibilities

By Nikki Hillhouse

Life has a way of steering us toward unexpected paths, often in ways we could never predict. At the time, they may feel overwhelming, like insurmountable obstacles placed in our path to hold us back. But in hindsight, we often see that they were guiding us toward something greater, something we might never have discovered without being pushed outside of our comfort zone.

My business journey was not a carefully laid-out plan with a clear roadmap to success. In fact, there was no plan at all, at least not in the traditional sense. It was born out of necessity, forged through adversity, and sustained by an unshakable belief that life had more to offer than simply surviving from one challenge to the next. It was a journey of resilience, self-discovery, and learning to trust that even the hardest moments were shaping me into the woman that I am today.

I never set out to be a business owner, a healer, a writer, or an international speaker. In the beginning, my focus was simply to rebuild my life after it had been turned upside down. From overcoming a stroke that could have defined me, to navigating the difficulties of being a young mother, to taking risks that felt terrifying, like starting my own business and later making the life-changing decision to move to Turkey, my story is one of trust.

A Life Interrupted

Life has a way of changing in an instant, and for me, that moment came when I suffered a stroke. I was young with a vision of how my future would unfold. Yet, in the blink of an eye, everything I had known, everything I had planned, was taken from me. The person I had been before the stroke felt like a distant memory, and I was left grappling with a reality I wasn't prepared for.

The physical toll was immense. My body, which had once carried me through life effortlessly, now felt foreign to me. Simple tasks became monumental challenges. I had to relearn movements I had once taken for granted. Every step forward required patience, perseverance, and a willingness to face the discomfort of the unknown. But the emotional and mental toll was just as profound. I struggled with frustration, grief, and the question that lingered in my mind: *Why did this happen to me?*

Doctors offered solutions in the form of medications. Their approach was focused on symptom management rather than true healing. I was prescribed medications to dull the pain and force my body into regulation to merely cope. But I craved more than survival; I was ready to thrive, seeking healing that went deeper than the physical. Deep down, I knew that true recovery couldn't come from a pill alone.

This realisation set me on a path of self-discovery and holistic healing. I began exploring alternative therapies, looking beyond conventional medicine for answers. I learned about the mind-body connection, about how trauma and stress could manifest physically, and about the profound impact that emotional healing could have on physical well-being. Meditation, energy healing, nutrition, yoga, and movement—each became a vital piece of my journey.

What started as a desperate search for my own healing soon evolved into something much bigger. As I pieced myself back together, I realised that my journey wasn't just about me. There were so many others struggling who felt trapped in their pain, lost in their circumstances, unsure of how to move forward. I couldn't ignore the pull I felt toward helping others find the healing I had discovered. My adversity had given me a purpose, and for the first time since my stroke, I felt a spark of hope for what lay ahead.

As I regained strength and deepened my knowledge of wellness, I knew that my journey wasn't just about my own healing; it was about helping others find relief from their own struggles. I had experienced firsthand how the body carries stress, trauma, and unprocessed emotions, and I understood that true healing had to go beyond just physical recovery. That's what led me to take my first step into entrepreneurship: becoming a massage therapist.

At the time, I had no formal background in business. I didn't have a detailed plan or a guidebook on how to build a successful practice. What I did have was an unshakable belief in the power of healing touch and a deep desire to make a difference in people's lives. I poured myself into learning everything I could and not just about massage techniques, but about how the body stores tension, how emotions manifest physically, and how therapeutic touch could help people reconnect with themselves on a deeper level.

Starting a business, however, was a whole new challenge. I had to figure out how to find clients, how to manage finances, how to build a brand, things I had never done before. There were moments of doubt, moments when I wondered if I had taken on too much. But every time I saw the relief in a client's face after a session, every time someone told me they finally felt at ease in their own body, I knew I was on the right path.

Many clients arrived burdened with stress, some with chronic pain, and emotional tension they didn't even realise they were carrying. They left lighter, freer, more in tune with themselves. Seeing that transformation reaffirmed my passion and gave me the confidence to keep going.

But life had more lessons in store for me. Entrepreneurship, like healing, is never a straight line. Just as I had to learn to navigate setbacks in my personal journey, I soon discovered that running a business came with its own set of challenges. There were highs and lows, unexpected obstacles, and moments that tested my resilience. Yet, through it all, I held onto the same lesson that had carried me through my own recovery: no matter how difficult things seemed, there was always a way forward.

Little did I know, my journey was only just beginning.

As I was building my business, I was also finding my way as a young mother navigating divorce, facing challenges of my own. But I knew one thing for sure, I wanted to show my son that no matter what life throws at you, hard work and perseverance open doors.

I didn't want him to grow up seeing adversity as a dead end. Instead, I wanted him to see that setbacks can be stepping stones. It wasn't just about making a living; it was about creating a legacy for him, showing him that dreams are worth fighting for.

Paying Forward as a Catalyst for Growth

I felt an undeniable pull to give back. It wasn't enough to focus solely on my own journey. I wanted to be of service to others who were struggling, whether they were dealing with chronic pain, emotional trauma, or simply feeling lost in life. There was something deeply fulfilling about offering support without expectation, about reaching out to those who needed guidance, encouragement, or even just a listening ear.

Volunteer work became a crucial part of my personal and professional growth. It wasn't just an act of kindness; it was a way for me to deepen my understanding of healing in all its forms. I worked with various organisations, offering my skills to children and adult hospices and those who wouldn't normally have access to holistic wellness practices. Whether it was providing massage therapy, coaching individuals through emotional challenges, running my meditation classes, or simply being present for someone in need, I saw firsthand how healing extends far beyond the physical.

Each person I worked with had a story, a struggle, a pain they carried. Some had endured immense hardship, whether it was physical illness, abuse, financial difficulties, or the weight of unhealed emotional wounds. I saw how suffering often disconnected people from themselves, how trauma created barriers that kept them stuck. But I also saw something else, hope. Even in the darkest moments, there was a spark within each person, a small but powerful force that, when nurtured, could help them rebuild their lives.

Through volunteering, I realised that true healing is holistic; it's not just about alleviating physical symptoms, but about addressing the emotional, mental, and spiritual aspects of a person's well-being. No amount of massage therapy, coaching, meditation, or medical treatment could bring lasting change if deeper wounds remain unhealed. This understanding shaped my approach to wellness in a profound way.

I no longer saw healing as something I provided to people. Instead, I saw it as something I helped them *reclaim* for themselves. My role wasn't to *"fix"* anyone but to empower them to recognise their own inner strength, to reconnect with the wisdom within them, and to take charge of their own healing journey.

Through kind words, support, or inspiration, volunteering became a cycle of giving and receiving, where every person I helped also helped me grow in ways I hadn't expected. It reinforced my belief that we are all connected, that our struggles and triumphs are intertwined, and that by lifting others, we also rise.

This desire to serve stayed with me as my journey evolved. It wasn't just something I did on the side; it became part of the foundation of my work. And as I expanded my vision for the future, I knew that giving back would always be at the heart of everything I created.

I later expanded my practice by studying and qualifying in nutritional science and therapeutic techniques focused on uncovering and resolving the root causes of health issues and life challenges. By integrating this knowledge with my holistic approaches, I found an even more effective way to support my clients on their healing journeys.

Taking a Leap of Faith

As my business grew, so did my vision. I had spent hours working with people one-on-one, helping them release pain, process emotions, and reconnect with their bodies. But I knew there was something more waiting for me, something bigger than just individual sessions. I wanted to create a space where people could fully immerse themselves in healing, away from the distractions and demands of everyday life. A sanctuary. A place where transformation could unfold in a deeper, more profound way.

That dream led me to Turkey.

The idea of moving to a new country, of starting over yet again, could have been overwhelming. But this time, it felt different. It felt like the natural next step, like my entire journey had been leading me here. And in many ways, the decision was made easier because we already had a house in Turkey. Having that foundation gave me a sense of security, a place to land as I took this bold leap. It wasn't just about escaping or chasing a dream; it was about stepping into a reality I had been building for years.

I could see it so clearly in my mind: retreats nestled in nature, where people could come together to heal, reconnect, and transform. A space filled with warmth, support, and laughter, where they could shed the weight of their past and rediscover their own strength. I envisioned mornings filled with meditation and movement, afternoons of deep healing work, and evenings where stories were shared under the stars. I wasn't just creating a business; I was creating a haven for the soul.

Of course, stepping into the unknown is never without its challenges. There were moments of doubt, moments where I questioned whether I was really ready to take this risk. But I wasn't doing it alone. Throughout this journey, I had the unwavering support of my partner, who believed in my vision as much as I did. He stood by me through every decision, every late-night planning session, every moment of uncertainty. When I wavered, he reminded me why I was doing this. When the doubts crept in, he reassured me that I was capable, that this dream was not only possible but inevitable.

That support made all the difference. It gave me the confidence to take that leap not just with hope, but with trust. Trust in myself, in my journey, in the belief that everything I had experienced up until this point had prepared me for what was coming next.

So, I did it. I left behind the familiarity of my old life and embraced the unknown. I stepped into the vision I had held in my heart for so long, trusting that it would unfold exactly as it was meant to. And as I stood in our home in Turkey, looking out at the landscape that would soon become a sanctuary for healing, I knew, without a doubt, that I had made the right choice.

Embracing the Journey of Growth

As my retreats gained traction and my story spread, something completely unexpected happened. I was invited to speak at an international summit for inspirational women.

I was shocked. Me? A speaker?

I had spent years helping others heal, but standing on a stage and sharing my story with the world wasn't something I had ever planned for. Yet, here I was, invited to speak at the Women's Thrive Summit, sharing my journey of transformation, resilience, and entrepreneurship.

That moment changed everything. Speaking in front of an audience of incredible women made me realise that my story had the power to inspire far beyond my coaching and retreats. It wasn't just about wellness; it was about showing women that they could rewrite their own stories, no matter what they had been through.

That summit was a turning point. It opened doors I never even knew existed, leading to collaborations, authorship, and the realisation that my voice, my truth, could help others step into their power.

Building a Business with Purpose

Through all of this, I stayed grounded in my mission: to help people heal, reclaim their power, and live a life of freedom.

Entrepreneurship, for me, was never just about business. It was about impact. It was about creating something meaningful, something that aligned with my values of integrity, honesty, love, and freedom.

I built my business not just through strategy, but through intention. Every retreat, every coaching session, was infused with the lessons I had learned about healing, about resilience, about stepping into the fullest version of yourself.

And I knew that this was just the beginning.

Embracing My Legacy

Looking back, I see that every challenge, every struggle, every moment of doubt was leading me to this exact place.

The stroke, living with chronic pain, the divorce, the uncertainty of starting a business, the fear of stepping onto a stage, all of it was shaping me into the entrepreneur, healer, and speaker I am today.

I once thought my adversities were obstacles. Now, I see them as gifts. They gave me the strength, wisdom, and courage to build something extraordinary, not just for myself, but for every person I have had the privilege of helping.

I share my story not to say, "Look what I've done," but to say, "Look what's possible."

Because if I can do it, so can you.

Nikki Hillhouse
nikkihillhouse.com

Kimberly Tyler

https://www.linkedin.com/in/kimberly-tyler-a8849539/
https://www.facebook.com/profile.php?id=100094747320115
https://www.instagram.com/brokenvesselholylight/
www.brokenvesselholylight.com

Kimberly Tyler, M.Ed, is an international best-selling author with over 30 years of experience in education and children's ministry leadership. A retired educational administrator, she possesses a wealth of knowledge and experience in student success through positive learning environments and advocacy of inclusive practices. Kimberly is an inspiring author with a profound gift for seeing others succeed despite any challenges that they may face. Residing in Northern California on an urban homestead with her husband and extended family, she draws inspiration from the beautiful surroundings and close-knit community. Kimberly's writing reflects her genuine desire to uplift and empower readers as she shares stories that resonate with faith, hope, and resilience. Her unique blend of storytelling and encouragement has positively impacted the hearts of readers worldwide. An accomplished creative, her favorite mediums are fabric arts such as quilting and embroidery.

Answering the Calling of Entrepreneurship

By Kimberly Tyler

The First Step Is the Hardest

Starting something new can feel like stepping off a cliff—you can't quite see the ground beneath you, but something deep inside tells you to leap. That's how it felt when I first said yes to writing. I didn't have a platform. I didn't have a following. I didn't fully believe I was "qualified" to be an author. But I had a story in my heart and a stirring, a calling I couldn't ignore, and I knew it was time to begin.

Looking back now, I realize that saying yes was one of the bravest decisions I've ever made. Not because I had everything figured out, but because I didn't. All I had was the willingness to try and a deep trust that God would meet me in the unknown. And He did—every single step.

This chapter is for the woman who's been holding onto a dream but hasn't known where to start. It's for the author who's written the words but wonders if anyone will ever read them. It's for the entrepreneur in the making who needs a little reminder that small beginnings can lead to great things.

Friend, if that's you, let me gently say that you are not alone. You don't have to have all the answers to begin. You have to be willing to take that first step. And when you do, you'll find that the path begins to unfold beneath your feet.

Let this be your invitation—and your inspiration—to start walking. You never know who might be waiting on the other side of your "yes."

The Spark That Lit the Fire

There's something beautiful about beginnings. They don't usually come wrapped in clarity and confidence. They come wrapped in questions and what-ifs. What if I fail? What if no one reads it? What if I'm not cut out for this?

But they also carry the kind of hope that only fresh starts can bring. That first "yes" lit a fire I didn't know I had. It wasn't about being famous or getting rich but about answering a calling to share what God had placed in my heart. And once that fire was lit, I couldn't ignore it.

At first, I said yes quietly. I contributed to a collaboration book and watched nervously as it went out into the world. And to my surprise, it resonated—not just with friends and family but with strangers who saw pieces of their own story in mine. That's when I began to understand: Your words can carry light into places you've never even seen.

Each opportunity that followed helped me grow—not just as a writer but as a woman learning to trust her voice. The spark became a steady flame, and I realized this wasn't a one-time thing. This was the beginning of something God-planted and purpose-filled—something worth pursuing with all my heart.

And here's what I've learned since: When God ignites something in you, it might start as a spark—but if you keep saying yes, it can become a wildfire of purpose, passion, and joy that touches more lives than you ever imagined.

When the Money Doesn't Match the Mission

Let me say something honest here—being a bestselling author doesn't mean you're making a full-time income. I learned that the hard way. After the initial excitement of release day faded and the supportive rush of friends and family buying my book passed, reality set in. Sales slowed. Income was inconsistent. And the question came: How do I make this more than a one-time success?

It was humbling but also clarifying. It forced me to ask myself why I was doing this. Was it for applause? Or was it for the woman on the other side of the page who needed to hear that she wasn't alone? That God had a plan for her life? That she could start over?

I realized then that success wouldn't come just from book sales. It would come from the impact those words had on others and the relationships I built through them. And if I wanted to grow, I would need to learn how to steward this calling well—not just creatively, but also practically.

I started researching and asking questions. I humbled myself and admitted that I didn't know how to turn this passion into profit yet, but I was willing to learn because I believed in the message and the mission.

There were moments I felt discouraged, watching others seem to soar ahead while I was still figuring things out. But I reminded myself: This is my path, and I can walk it at my own pace. The mission is still worth it, even when the finances haven't caught up. Because obedience always bears fruit, even if we don't see the harvest immediately.

Learning to Share Your Voice

When I started showing up online, I had to get brave in a whole new way. Creating a Facebook page felt like a big deal. Posting my first Instagram photo? Nerve-wracking. I wasn't used to putting myself out there. I didn't know how to make a reel or write authentic captions. I was more comfortable behind the scenes, writing quietly and praying the words would reach whoever needed them.

But I also knew this: I had to be willing to be seen if I wanted to grow.

So, I took a deep breath and started. I shared a simple post with a verse that had encouraged me. I told a story about a time I almost quit. I celebrated small wins and admitted big fears. And what surprised me most? People responded. Not just with likes or emojis but with real words. "Thank you for sharing this." "I needed this today." "You put into words what I've been feeling."

That's when it clicked: marketing isn't about performing but connecting. Social media isn't just a platform; it's a bridge.

And that bridge? It has led to friendships, prayer partners, beta readers, and ministry opportunities. I'm learning that consistency matters more than perfection. That honesty builds more trust than polished posts ever could. And that your voice—yes, *yours*—has the power to bring light and healing to someone else's day.

Building a Home Online

Eventually, I knew I needed a place where all of this could live—a home base for my books, blog, and journey. So, I built a website.

Let me be clear: I had no idea what I was doing. I didn't know the first thing about domains, templates, or how to make things "look professional." But I took a deep breath and started learning—watching tutorials, reading articles, and asking questions. Slowly, piece by piece, it came together.

There's something powerful about claiming your space—digitally and spiritually. That website became more than just a place to sell books. It became a declaration: I'm here. I'm doing the thing. I'm showing up for myself and others.

Creating a website gave me freedom—freedom to share what was on my heart, showcase the books I'd poured my soul into, and encourage women who stumbled upon my page at just the right time. It gave me a voice outside of social media—something I could grow at my own pace, in my own way.

It's still evolving, and that's okay. Websites, like dreams, grow in layers. And with every blog post I publish or new page I build, I feel a little more rooted in the work I'm called to do.

Growing Into the Entrepreneurial Mindset

Somewhere along the way, I realized that being an author wasn't the end goal—it was the beginning. I was building something more significant than a book. I was stepping into entrepreneurship.

That realization came with both excitement and responsibility. Writing was my heart, but building a business? That was new territory. I had to learn to talk about my work in a way that invited others in, without feeling like I was "selling" something. I had to think about how to market what I'd created, price my books, and package my story in a way that honored both the message and the mission.

And perhaps most importantly, I had to give myself permission to succeed.

For so long, I thought ministry and money couldn't walk hand in hand. But I've come to understand that it's okay to want your calling to be sustainable. It's okay to dream of turning your passion into your profession. You're not less spiritual for wanting to steward your gift well—you're being wise.

The more I learn, the more empowered I feel. It's not about chasing algorithms or trends—it's about building a brand with heart. A brand that reflects who I am, what I believe, and how I hope to serve.

Supporting Other Women on the Journey

One of the most beautiful parts of this journey has been the people I've met along the way, especially the women. Women who are chasing dreams, writing books, starting businesses, and stepping out in faith with trembling hands but determined hearts. There's something sacred about walking this road together.

I've learned that we don't need to compete; we need to connect. We're not called to build empires—we're called to build each other up. And when we do, something powerful happens. We create safe spaces for dreams to grow and remind one another that we're not crazy about pursuing something that hasn't fully unfolded yet.

Some of my most significant growth has come from conversations with other women on this path. We've shared struggles, celebrated milestones, exchanged tips and resources, and prayed for each other through discouragement. These moments remind me that success isn't just about what we accomplish—it's also about who we bring along with us.

If I can support one more woman to say yes to her dream, then every lesson I've learned is worth it. Because when we rise together, we rise stronger.

Dreaming Forward—What's Next?

So, where am I headed?

Honestly, I'm still discovering that day by day—but what's different now is that I'm no longer afraid to dream big. I've walked far enough to see that even the smallest steps lead to beautiful places when taken in faith. I'm beginning to see how all the pieces—writing, ministry, entrepreneurship, and connection—can come together to create something meaningful, lasting, and deeply impactful.

I dream of writing more books—books that speak to the heart, minister to the weary, and remind women that they are never too far gone for God to use. I see devotionals and guided journals as resources women can hold in their hands and return to again and again. I imagine creating online courses, workshops, and digital spaces where women can gather, grow, and be equipped—not just to dream but to build.

More and more, I feel called to help others find their voice and use it with confidence. I don't want to just write—I want to empower. To help women who are where I once was—uncertain, unseen, and unsure where to begin—to believe that their message matters and that their journey has a purpose. I picture coaching groups, writing retreats, and perhaps even a membership community for faith-driven creatives and entrepreneurs.

But even as I dream big, I'm learning to hold those dreams loosely. I've discovered that God often unfolds the vision in stages. He doesn't always hand us the whole map—sometimes, He gives us the next step. And that's okay because with each obedient "yes," the picture becomes clearer.

I've also learned that dreaming forward means being willing to let go of comparison. My journey won't look like hers, and hers won't look like mine. And that's the beauty of it. There is space for all of us to thrive in our own calling. There is room at the table, and better yet—we're invited to help build it.

The dream ahead isn't about popularity or perfection. It's about faithfulness. It's about using every tool, every lesson, every opportunity to glorify God and serve others with what's been placed in our hands.

So, I'll keep dreaming, keep building, and keep trusting the process. Because the journey isn't finished—it's just getting started.

And if you're standing at the edge of your own "what's next," let this be your reminder: Don't be afraid to dream forward. God is already in your tomorrow, and He's prepared the way for you to walk.

If you're reading this and thinking, *I want to start, but I'm scared,* let me tell you—so was I. I still am sometimes. But courage isn't the absence of fear. It's deciding that your calling matters more than your comfort. And the beautiful truth is, you don't have to have it all figured out to take that first step.

You don't need a giant following. You don't need a perfect website. You don't need all the answers. You just need a willing heart and a message that won't let you stay silent. God does His best work in surrendered hearts and small beginnings. He's not waiting for you to be polished—He's just waiting for you to say yes.

The journey ahead may not be easy, but it will be worth it. You'll grow. You'll stumble. You'll celebrate and learn and stretch in ways you never imagined. And through it all, you'll find joy in the becoming. Because entrepreneurship, at its core, is a journey of becoming— becoming bold, becoming faithful, becoming the woman God created you to be.

So, here's your invitation: Start. Write the blog. Launch the idea. Share the story. Be seen. Let your light shine.

Your voice matters. Your story matters. And this world is waiting for the light that only *you* can shine.

Step forward. Trust the One who called you. Your path begins right here.

And I'll be cheering for you every step of the way.

Susan Tatem

Founder and CEO of Bright Path Coaching
Coach & Author

https://www.facebook.com/SusanMTatem
https://www.instagram.com/susanmtatem/
https://brightpath4autism.org

CEO of Bright Path Coaching, Author, Healthcare Provider, and Managing Partner for She Wins Women's Network Susan Tatem, the founder of Bright Path Coaching, is dedicated to empowering families of children with autism 12 years and older to navigate school and the transition into independent adulthood. Inspired by her own journey as a single mom raising a daughter with autism, Susan combines personal experience, professional expertise from 30 years in healthcare, and a deep passion to guide families with compassion and clarity. Her coaching provides parents with the tools to create a clear path for their children's future, addressing challenges like workforce readiness, independent living, and social skills. Susan's ultimate vision is to establish supported living communities worldwide, where young adults with autism can thrive. With honesty, integrity, and a heart for service, Bright Path Coaching equips families to transform worry into confidence, ensuring every individual with autism has the opportunity to lead a fulfilled, independent life. Additionally, Susan is the Managing Partner of the Tidewater Virginia Chapter of the She Wins Women's Network. She Wins is all about empowering women entrepreneurs and professionals to connect, collaborate, and grow. It's a space where we can build meaningful relationships, elevate our businesses, and truly thrive shoulder to shoulder. Let's rise and win together!

Strength in the Struggle: Finding My Path, My Voice, and My Vision

By Susan Tatem

If you had told me five years ago that I'd be hosting my own TV show, speaking in front of people, and coaching families of children with autism—while still working full-time in healthcare—I would've laughed. Or cried. Or both. But here I am, standing in a purpose I never could've imagined when I was deep in the trenches of survival mode.

My name is Susan Tatem, and I'm a mother, a coach, an advocate, a speaker, a wife, and a woman who has fought her way through pain, fear, trauma, and uncertainty to create a life that finally aligns with the calling in my heart. This is the story of how I got here—from heartbreak and self-doubt to standing in my truth and building a business that helps others walk their own path to a brighter, fulfilling future.

I grew up believing I wasn't enough. Not pretty enough. Not thin enough. Not strong enough. No matter what I did or how hard I tried, I never measured up—especially in the eyes of the people who were supposed to love me most.

Verbal abuse was the soundtrack of my childhood. Being called "fat" and "ugly" was a label that stuck to my soul and shaped how I saw myself for decades. I spent years trying to earn love and approval, especially from my parents. I just wanted them to be proud of me. I tried everything to make that happen, but it always felt like I came up short.

I was stuck in a cycle of trying to prove my worth, while never truly believing I had any. But life doesn't wait for us to heal. In the middle of that pain, I became a mom—and not just any mom, but the single mother of a daughter with special needs. That transformed me in ways I never expected.

From the beginning, I knew my daughter's path wouldn't look like everyone else's. And I also knew one thing for certain: as her mom, I would move mountains for her. I became her advocate, her voice, her researcher, her therapist, her teacher, and her safe place. I dove into every resource I could find. I asked questions. I demanded answers. I didn't stop. My daughter became my why. My life. My fight. My fire. I stepped into a world I had no training for but every instinct to navigate.

And while I poured my heart and soul into my daughter and the autism community, I held down a full-time job in healthcare. I was showing up for patients, managing my job, and carrying the weight of single motherhood, often with a broken spirit and a worn-out body. I was juggling all the roles, and still battling the old voices in my head telling me I wasn't enough. But here's the thing—when your child needs you, you find a way. You *become* the way. Failure is not an option. So, I wiped the tears off my face, took a deep breath, and told myself, *You got this!*

There were nights when I collapsed into bed with tears soaking the pillow before I even had time to pray. I was doing everything for everyone, and yet... sometimes there was still that quiet voice of desperation in me that said, *But what about you?* For a long time, I silenced it. I told myself my dreams didn't matter anymore. That it was selfish to want something for myself when my daughter needed so much. Now, I see it differently.

I was exhausted. Not just physically from the demands of my job, but emotionally as well. I had recovered from a broken ankle but was now dealing with more health issues, including pinched nerves in my lower back. I needed something uplifting—something that wasn't about surviving, but *living*. I wanted to build a future where I wasn't tied to someone else's schedule or limited by someone else's belief in what I was worth. I wanted peace. I wanted my time back. I wanted to just breathe. That shift wouldn't come until years later.

A few years ago, I found myself in a space I never imagined: staring at a screen, signing up to start an online travel agency. So, I jumped in. I partnered with a company that promised freedom, flexibility, and financial growth. I was told I'd be mentored and trained. I believed it, but the truth hit fast and hard. My so-called "mentor" told me that mentoring just made people dependent on him. That stung. I didn't want to be dependent—I just wanted to learn.

I remember closing my laptop one night, tears burning behind my eyes, whispering to myself, *Is it me? Am I just not good enough or smart enough for this?* That voice—the one that had haunted me since childhood—was creeping back in: *You're not good enough. You'll never make it. Just quit.* But I didn't want to quit. So I did something brave. I hired a sales coach.

What I got was so much more. She asked me questions no one had ever asked. About my mindset. My beliefs. My fears. My relationship with money. I started to realize—I wasn't just building a business. I was rebuilding myself.

For the first time in my life, I saw the way I belittled and underestimated myself. The way I let depression, anxiety, and fear lead. The way I had internalized every insult, every rejection, every dismissal. And I started asking myself, *What do I really want? Who do I need to become to facilitate the life I want?*

That's when the lightbulb came on. I wanted to become a coach and help women—like me—find love and happiness like I did in a crazy, confusing, cruel world. I thought, *Yes. I can do this. I can help others find what I've found and be as happy as I am.*

So, I launched my first coaching business. I was proud of it and of myself. I learned how to post content. I created a website and an e-book. I made business cards. I joined Facebook groups where my niche clients were. But... something was missing. Every time I hit a bump or got stuck, something in me whispered, *Can I really do this? This isn't it. This isn't the work you're meant to do.*

I ignored it at first. I told myself I was just afraid, just doubting. But deep down, I knew. I felt the passion slowly fade because the truth was... my heart was somewhere else entirely. This is not what lights me up inside, what I could go on and on about for days with total strangers.

I wanted it to work—the relationship coaching business. I really did.

I poured myself into it. I showed up, created content, talked about dating, swiped through apps, and tried to help women find love in a world that often feels unkind and confusing. I was doing the work, saying the right things, following the strategies I had learned.

But every time I sat down to write or coach, something felt off. Like I was wearing someone else's shoes—almost the right size, but not quite. I kept trying to push that feeling aside. *You're just nervous, Susan. Give it time. This is what you asked for.*

But my spirit knew.

And one day, I got word that my autism advocate had passed away. Her name was Rachel. She was so instrumental in shaping both my daughter's life and mine. Without her guidance, support, and accountability, I surely would have helicopter mom'd my daughter into a dependent lifestyle without even realizing it. I owed so much to her—and she never expected anything in return.

That was it! I couldn't ignore it anymore. I sat in silence with my journal open, the pen shaking in my hand, and I wrote the words I'd been too afraid to say out loud: *I don't want to do this anymore.*

I went back to the stage of the course I was going through with my sales coach, who had changed her niche to helping people start their own coaching business. She had a tool that asked you questions and walked you through the steps to discovering your passion, your niche. The answer came like a rolling thunder—but it hit like lightning: *I want to help families like mine. I want to be their Rachel. I want to serve by sharing everything I've already learned and lived through.*

I remember just sitting there... stunned. *Why hadn't I seen it before?* I finally gave myself permission to stop trying to build someone else's dream, and start answering the call that had been planted inside me all along. *This is what lights me up.* Always has been.

I looked at my own life—decades of living in the trenches, advocating, leading, supporting, showing up. I didn't have to fabricate a brand-new identity. I *was* the niche. My life experience *was* the certification.

That's when I pivoted. I stopped forcing what didn't fit and started building what felt like home. I created a coaching business to help families of children with autism carve out a clear path to guide their child into the future—not just through school, but into adulthood. Because I knew what it was like to lie awake at night wondering, *What will happen when I'm gone? Will she be able to live on her own? What about driving? Working?*

But even more than the niche, I found something else—I found my *calling.* My voice. My *vision.* My *why.* And when I tell you that changed everything, I mean **everything.**

Entrepreneurship is often romanticized—portrayed as a bold leap into freedom, passion, and prosperity. But the reality, especially for women like me who are building while still tethered to a demanding full-time job and managing complex health challenges, is far more intricate. The leap is not one big moment; it is a thousand small, intentional steps taken in between physical pain, mental exhaustion, and the ticking of a clock that never seems to stop.

Time was my greatest constraint. Every hour outside of my healthcare job felt borrowed. I wasn't starting a business in a vacuum—I was still showing up for patients during the day, still managing a household, helping my young adult daughter, and learning how to build a happy marriage with the love of my life. That meant every moment spent on my business had to be strategic. Planned. Intentional. I learned to optimize small windows of time: an early morning before the shift, a quiet evening when the house was finally still, weekends carved out with precision. Time, for me, became both currency and battleground.

For years, I felt like my 9–5 job was holding me hostage. I was grateful for it—I needed the paycheck, the stability, the benefits—but it drained me. I resented it. I blamed it. So, I flipped the narrative. I started viewing it as a tool. *This job works for me now. I no longer serve it—it serves me.*

But the physical toll couldn't be ignored. Years of labor-intensive work had left my body weary. Chronic back pain from pinched nerves often made it hard to walk, sit, or stand for any length of time. A broken ankle. Major shoulder surgery. Some days, even getting out of bed was pure mind over matter. My body was asking for rest, but my drive was demanding progress. My life now had a purpose that was much bigger than me. If I wanted to reach people all over the world to help them, I needed to consistently show up no matter what.

On top of all that, I was navigating the invisible battles—depression, anxiety, and a mind conditioned by years of verbal and emotional abuse. The voices that told me I wasn't good enough didn't just disappear when I started a business. If anything, they got louder. Every time I tried something new, fear would rise up like an old friend wearing a new disguise. *Who do you think you are? Why would anyone listen to you? You're going to fail—again.*

I kept going not because I didn't hear the fear, but because I leaned into it. I embraced mindset coaching. I made the conscious decision to dismantle the false beliefs that had kept me small for so long. I committed to the mantra of think small, get small but think big, get big.

Stepping into my empowered self was a difficult and daily process. Perhaps the hardest decision I made was cutting ties with the very people whose approval I had spent my whole life chasing. For three years, I didn't speak to my mother. It was one of the most painful decisions I've ever made—but also one of the most necessary. I had to remove the poison, no matter what shape it came in, if I was ever going to fully heal and grow.

This season of my journey was not glamorous. It was exhausting but also sacred. For the first time in my life, I had the most amazing husband beside me, loving me, supporting me, and believing in me. Never could I have ever imagined a life like this for me.

I reclaimed my energy—not because the circumstances changed, but because *I* did.

I used my income to fund the tools I needed. I invested in coaching. I created systems. I paid for the things that would give me *time*, because time is one of the most precious things an entrepreneur can buy. And here's the beautiful part: I wasn't hustling from a place of scarcity anymore—I was building from a place of strategy and alignment. That's when things started to take off.

There's something powerful about no longer needing anyone else to validate your worth. I still work full-time in healthcare. I still deal with chronic pain, and yes—fear still sneaks in from time to time, whispering its old lies. But I am no longer that woman who believed she wasn't enough. I don't chase approval anymore. I stand rooted in purpose.

I am a published author.

A managing partner of a local chapter for the She Wins Women's

Network.

A speaker who shares her story to empower others.

A host of my own TV show on a streaming platform.

And I am an autism coach—walking in the very calling that's been burning deep inside me for over two decades.

I look at the woman I've become and see someone who rose from trauma, silence, and self-doubt and chose *impact* over fear. I see someone who could have given up—so many times—but kept going, one quiet, brave step at a time.

Do I still have hard days? Yes.

Do I still feel overwhelmed? Absolutely.

But now I have tools. I have vision. And most importantly, I found *me*.

Maureen Byers GRI

Master of Real Estate & National Innovator

https://www.linkedin.com/in/maureen-b-63938997
https://www.facebook.com/share/1AxVaGqnER/
https://www.instagram.com/byersmaureen
https://wa.me/+18584137887

Maureen Byers is a pioneering force in Colorado, Arizona, and California real estate. Starting as a single mother relying on assistance, she transformed her life into that of a successful broker, investor, and entrepreneur. With an advanced education and extensive experience facilitating high-value real estate transactions, Maureen specializes in commercial investment, creative financing, and property development. As a 1031 tax-deferred exchanger and seller financing expert, she skillfully navigates complex transactions for a global clientele. Her entrepreneurial spirit led her to establish a brokerage where she has represented and supported aspiring real estate professionals. Maureen's approach combines hard work with innovative strategies she learned along her journey, allowing her to embrace her uniqueness and authenticity. She believes true achievement is not just measured by financial milestones but by the ability to inspire others and help them reach their goals. Today, Maureen leads a vibrant real estate investment network dedicated to empowering individuals in their pursuit of financial independence.

Unlock Your Real Estate Potential with Expert Guidance

By Maureen Byers GRI

Embarking on an entrepreneurial journey in real estate has been one of the most rewarding and challenging experiences of my life. I was initially drawn to this field as a single mother in college, seeking a stable career. My choices were narrowed down to two passions: real estate and gemology. Ultimately, I chose real estate, which has provided me with the opportunity to create a fulfilling life for myself and my family and to become a role model for others.

From navigating the complexities of the market to learning invaluable lessons from industry leaders, every step has shaped my approach to investing. In this chapter, I share key insights, lessons learned, and the resources that have inspired me along the way. Whether you're a seasoned investor or just starting, I hope my experiences resonate with you and motivate you to pursue your own journey in real estate.

Current Market Conditions

Understanding the current real estate market conditions is crucial for making informed decisions. Here's a brief overview of the market status in key states:

State	Market Type
Colorado	Neutral
Arizona	Buyer's Market
California	Seller's Market

Lessons Learned

1. Invest in Yourself:

Investing in myself has been the cornerstone of my entrepreneurial journey. Early on, I recognized the importance of education and mentorship. I attended numerous events and sought guidance from experienced professionals. One pivotal moment was when I enrolled in a real estate investment course that opened my eyes to new strategies. This investment enhanced my knowledge and expanded my network, leading to opportunities I never imagined.

Personal Story: The decision to start my own business instead of working for someone else was a pivotal moment in my life. Though I found myself responsible for my business at every level, which can be overwhelming, the rewards have far outweighed the challenges. Real estate is in my blood; I feel a deep connection to it. As a broker, partner, investor, and entrepreneur, I've discovered that my purpose is to help others realize their dreams. Providing clients with financing, resources, and connections to succeed has been incredibly fulfilling. Even when faced with setbacks, I bounce back, learning from my mistakes and continuing to create and provide valuable services to others. Ultimately, this journey has taught me to love where I live, enjoy coming home, and be grateful for the impact I can have on the lives of others.

2. Embrace Resilience:

Resilience has been tested time and again throughout my career. I recall a period when the market took a downturn, and many of my clients faced financial hardships. Instead of succumbing to despair, I reassessed my strategies and found new ways to support my clients. This experience taught me that every setback is an opportunity for growth.

Personal Story: Being the only woman in a commercial investment brokerage, becoming a resort specialist, and listing a multi-million dollar property in the mountains of Colorado was both challenging and rewarding. At just 25 years old, I was the listing and selling broker, which would be valued at millions of dollars today. It took me a year to sell the property and a lot of commuting from Denver to the Colorado Rockies. I listed, marketed, toured, sold, and closed the entire town of Almont, Colorado, including the real estate, the PUC licenses for rafting on the contiguous river, on-site businesses, lodge, liquor and general store, bar and restaurant, cabin rentals, and main home.

3. Networking Is Key:

Building relationships has been instrumental to my success. I remember attending a networking event where I met a mentor who guided me through significant career decisions. This connection led to collaborations that transformed my business. I've learned that every person you meet has the potential to change your trajectory.

Personal Story: Networking is the foundation of your business, and those relationships and referrals are worth their weight in gold. Sometimes, you become friends with your clients, and I have friends that I've had for over 40 years who started out as clients and became friends. My brother knew that I had just gotten married in Chicago and asked me to come out and meet developers from Arizona and Nevada who had a large project in Southwest Colorado. They hired me as their on-site broker to run the project. I purchased properties and provided private financing for reselling to offer affordability to those who had compromised credit. I partnered on some of the properties for new construction or renovation. I brought in a major builder from Southern California to build homes for my clientele.

4. Balance Is Critical:

Finding a balance between work and personal life is essential for long-term success. I've often pushed myself to the limits, only to realize that neglecting my health and well-being led to burnout. Prioritizing self-care and scheduling time for maintaining a regular, active, and social lifestyle, meditation, and family has made me a more effective entrepreneur.

Personal Story: I have found it challenging to maintain balance at work since I consider myself a workaholic, which has led to chronic bronchitis and pneumonia. I realized that maintaining balance among family, friends, health, faith, business, and personal well-being is crucial. I've learned that self-love and the science of letting go are essential, along with a balanced diet, exercise, hydration, sleep, and a routine that limits drama and enhances life's pleasures.

5. Say Yes to Opportunities:

One of the most transformative lessons I've learned is to say yes to new experiences. I vividly recall the moment I agreed to speak at a local real estate summit. Despite my initial fears, that experience opened doors to new clients and collaborations. Embracing opportunities—even those that push you out of your comfort zone—can lead to remarkable outcomes.

Personal Story: Formerly, a board panel member of the The National Association of Realtors serving on The Professional Standards Board, Grievance and Mediation Committees, Master of Real Estate Task Force, International Council of Real Estate, Women's Real Estate Council, Costa Rica Board and Arizona New Mexico Commission representing Real Estate brokers at the Round Table with a real estate attorney, real estate CPA, real estate developer, and real estate financier. These experiences provided exponential growth, confidence, and understanding that reinforced my authenticity and powerful authority. Being witnessed by others, feeling alive and making a difference, and not only my perception but also enjoying the bigger picture and changing lives, always put a smile on my face, even though at times we have to face our fears. We have our faith to carry us through and start anew every single day, just like the sun rising and setting or the waves crashing the shoreline and returning to sea calmly. As a boogie boarder in the water closer to the shore before the breaks, I have learned to have a broad sweeping vision of the ocean on any given day, which is different, and to plan to accept and expect the changes that I choose to ride certain waves.

6. Adaptability Is Essential:

The real estate market is constantly evolving, and my ability to adapt has been crucial to my success. I remember a time when technology began to revolutionize the industry. Instead of resisting change, I embraced it by learning about new tools and platforms, allowing me to stay relevant and serve my clients better.

Personal Story: The real estate market is cyclical, and after a slow recession during the 1990s, the market in Southwest Colorado dried up completely around 1999–2000. I had an opportunity to move to Arizona, where I got my real estate broker's license due to reciprocity with my home state. I rented a beautiful house in the Biltmore area, then moved to Scottsdale and ended up in Phoenix. This move allowed me to reconnect with my son as an investor and create a new partnership, while also starting a construction property maintenance management company to take care of our rentals. Living in the high desert was a beautiful experience, and I encourage everyone to embrace changes in their business, whether geographic or metaphysical.

7. Empower Others:

Throughout my journey, I've learned the importance of lifting others as I climb. I recall a woman who loved animals—she had several dogs and cats and was looking for a rental. When she contacted me, I asked if she had ever thought about buying her own home. She mentioned she probably wouldn't qualify, so I connected her with my lender, and to her surprise, she qualified! We went shopping together, exploring available rentals and homes for sale. I showed her a beautiful property in the historical district that had an extra lot, which I thought would be a great fit for her. When we closed escrow, I discovered she had a large number of pets that would not have been allowed in any rental. She has been forever grateful to me and continues to thrive in her new home.

Personal Story: By making the decision to become an entrepreneur and obtain the license, I was able to provide helicopter school for my son, help my sister and her children, and partner with my brother as a broker-investor. Together, we changed his life and income through real estate investments, providing stability for families and empowering women to become entrepreneurs by offering sponsorships and creative financing options.

Q&A Section

Q1: What inspired you to become an entrepreneur in the real estate industry?

A1: My inspiration stemmed from my passion for real estate and the desire to create opportunities for others. I wanted to provide value through expert guidance and build lasting relationships with clients. The thrill of helping someone find their dream property or achieve their investment goals is incredibly rewarding.

Q2: What are the biggest challenges you've faced as a woman in this industry?

A2: One of the biggest challenges has been overcoming stereotypes and biases that exist in a predominantly male-dominated field. However, these challenges have only strengthened my resolve to succeed and inspire other women to pursue their dreams in entrepreneurship and real estate.

Q3: How can someone just starting out in real estate gain credibility?

A3: Building credibility takes time and effort. Start by educating yourself—invest in courses, seek mentorship, and network with industry professionals. Sharing your knowledge and experiences through workshops or social media can also enhance your credibility within the community.

Q4: What is your advice for balancing work and personal life?

A4: Finding balance is crucial. Prioritize self-care and set boundaries to ensure you have time for both your business and personal life. Remember that taking breaks and caring for your health can ultimately enhance your productivity and effectiveness as an entrepreneur.

Q5: What resources do you recommend for aspiring real estate investors?

A5: I recommend books like *Rich Dad Poor Dad* by Robert Kiyosaki and *The Book on Rental Property Investing* by Brandon Turner. Additionally, online platforms like webinars, podcasts, and local real estate investment groups can provide valuable insights and learning opportunities.

Resources That Inspired My Journey

1. Books:

- Think and Grow Rich by Napoleon Hill
- Rich Dad Poor Dad by Robert Kiyosaki
- The 10X Rule by Grant Cardone
- The Closers by Jim Camp
- Success Through a Positive Mental Attitude by W. Clement Stone and Napoleon Hill
- The New Psycho-Cybernetics by Maxwell Maltz
- The Art of Closing the Sale by Brian Tracy

2. Mentors:

- Tom Hopkins: Renowned sales expert whose teachings on

selling have greatly influenced my approach to real estate.

- Donald Trump: His strategies in real estate development provided me with invaluable insights into the industry.
- Grant Cardone: His motivational approach has inspired me to think big and take action.
- Zig Ziglar: Motivational speaker and author known for his impactful teachings on sales and personal growth.
- W. Clement Stone: Entrepreneur and motivational speaker who emphasized the power of a positive attitude in achieving success.
- William "Bill" Bronchick: Expert in real estate investing, particularly known for creative financing and closing techniques.

3. Educational Programs:

- CCIM Institute: Completing my certificates has been a pivotal element in my real estate education.

Conclusion

As we conclude this journey together, I invite you to take the next step toward achieving your entrepreneurial aspirations. Whether you're just starting out in real estate or looking to expand your existing ventures, there is immense potential ahead of you.

Call to Action: Embrace your passion and take that first step. Follow your dreams, protect your peace, and pursue what brings you joy and fulfillment. Remember, "Follow your passion, and you'll be successful." Join me for my weekly Zoom sessions, where I provide valuable insights and support tailored to aspiring real estate investors. This is an opportunity to connect, learn, and grow within a community that values collaboration and empowerment.

Remember, success is within your reach. Embrace the opportunities that come your way, say "yes" to new experiences, and don't hesitate to reach out. Together, we can navigate the path to entrepreneurial growth and create a brighter future for ourselves and our communities.

For inquiries and to arrange a conversation, feel free to contact me directly:

Maureen Byers
WhatsApp: 858-413-7887
Email: oceansidemaureen@gmail.com
Zoom Link for Weekly Meetings: [Join the Zoom Session Here] (https://us06web.zoom.us/j/88258583346?pwd=99K6sQ08w1MK PC2SAlEJQD2LiBWt3P)

Meeting Details:
When: Every Thursday
Time: 4-5 p.m. PDT

Andrea C Russell

Founder of Journey to Business Success
Business Implementation & Financial Accountability Coach

www.linkedin.com/in/andrearussell1875
https://www.facebook.com/acrbookkeepingplus
https://www.instagram.com/christianwomenpreneur/
https://www.journeytobusinesssuccess.com
https://www.membership.andrearussellcoach.com

Andrea Russell isn't just another business coach; she's a lifeline for Christian Women Entrepreneurs drowning in the complexities of startup growth. With over 30 years of working with business owners, Andrea specializes in rescuing these passionate women from the brink of burnout. She understands that while you're skilled at your craft, navigating client acquisition and financial management can feel like deciphering a foreign language. What sets Andrea apart is her unique ability to blend strategic business planning with a deep understanding of Christian values, ensuring that every decision not only supports financial growth but also aligns with your spiritual mission. Her Business Clarity Collective Membership goes beyond traditional coaching by offering a community-focused, faith-based approach that encourages collaboration and learning. Join Andrea and discover how tailored coaching can transform your entrepreneurial journey, turning chaos into clarity and struggle into strategic growth. Embrace the support system designed to elevate your business and nourish your soul.

From Prayers to Profits: Crafting Your Business in God's Backyard

By Andrea C Russell

You wake up one morning, a dream still echoing in your mind like a catchy tune. There you were, playing a piano in an office building—only problem, you're no Beethoven. Puzzled by what it could mean, you jump online and discover the city has just opened a business incubator.

Fired up, you dash from work to check it out. The moment you step in, déjà vu hits—this was the very building from your dream!

"Is this for me?" you wonder.

Without overthinking it (because, really, who has time for that?), you sign the lease. Then, it hits you: You have an office, but not a single client.

"What have I done?" you think, panic brewing. But then, you remember Moses at the Red Sea, stick in hand, diving into the unknown because God said so. If Moses could step out in faith, why can't you?

Growing up, I wasn't just playing "store"—I lived it. Selling my first pastries at age 8, mimicking my entrepreneurial mom. Whether helping out at our family bakery, clothing store, or restaurant, business ran in my veins.

From those early mornings dropping my stepdad off at his painting job to helping mom prep the kitchen for her epic baking marathons—oh, and grating those stubborn coconuts—I soaked up the value of hard work and saw the ups and downs of running a business.

Mom always tried new recipes, and let me tell you, when a new recipe was in play, we'd be eating it for weeks! That was her secret sauce for making it perfect. This taught me to always strive for the best in everything I do.

Mom was a fountain of innovation. She believed in the power of persistence and perfecting our crafts, which instilled a drive in me that went beyond just participating—to excel in whatever I undertook.

Noticing my budding interest, my mom got me into a computer programming class right after high school in 1985. Binary numbers? At first, I thought, "Oh my goodness, I love numbers, but binary? What in the world does that mean?" It was all about computer languages. Loving a challenge, I dove in headfirst and loved it. That's where I fell in love with software, adding another piece to my business puzzle.

Fast forward through various ventures—a grocery store, a hosiery store, a shoe store, and a dollar store. I got the hang of opening and closing stores. It was like a game, seeing if I could do it. The part I loved most was winging the inventory and using my gut to figure out what would sell.

Guess what, like my step-dad always says, "God will bless the work of your hands." And he sure did! I had a knack for picking inventory, and customers would swoop in and buy everything.

It was all about showing me the money.

Each venture was my playground, testing my skills while balancing a day job and family. The fear of failure was real, but my drive was stronger.

"If God is for us, who can be against us?" (Romans 8:31). This verse kept me grounded, pushing me to go all-in on my business dreams after my daughter graduated high school.

In January 2015, I handed my boss the notice. My new chapter was set to start in August, right after I got my master's degree in accounting. But wait, there's more-

Hold your horses, because the story gets even better.

Two months after giving notice, I got a call. A gentleman had found my new bookkeeping firm online. I wasn't sure what to expect, but fear has no place in my business.

I walked by faith, not by sight, ready for any questions the potential client might have.

We met, and I nailed the proposal. Guess what? The contract was set to start in August—talk about divine timing!

A project meant to last just a few months turned into a seven-year client relationship. Imagine that—my clients are like family to me.

But to top it off, my boss kept me as a consultant for another six months.

God's timing? Impeccable.

Stepping out in faith with the right motives aligns with God's plan— well, it at least sorts out the schedule. We must be faithful and obedient, ready when the time comes.

"Faith without works is dead," James reminds us. And sure enough, the work began.

After signing the lease with no clients to speak of, I hustled to get QuickBooks certified and posted my profile online. Before I could second-guess my rates, a lead popped up.

A startup needed a full setup—my kind of challenge. She was an inventory-based store, right up my alley because I had the hefty task of managing inventory to the tune of $3M—ouch, talk about a lot!

I met with the potential client, gave her my price, and she paid in full, right on the spot. This client left after five years and came back a year later, so apologetic.

Being the kind heart I am, I couldn't say no. She has since passed away a few months ago, but her husband is still our client.

Growing a business is hard work, but we must remember our Why?

It's much more than just making money, while that is a big factor. For me, it's about helping my clients make a difference in their own lives and being able to support themselves, their families, and those around them.

Boom, lease paid.

Then another client signed on, and then another. It turns out, the biggest barrier is often the "what ifs" we throw in our path.

Armed with skills, a divine gift, and the Good Lord, I faced down my fears. My mantra? **"Failure is not an option,"** echoing through every decision.

"Whatever you do, work at it with all your heart, as working for the Lord, not for human masters." (Colossians 3:23) has been my guide.

This mindset has seen my clients go from startups to explosive growth.

Opening my dollar store was a leap of faith funded by modest savings and sheer grit. But as my mom used to say, **"Do it right or not at all."**

Here I am today, an **Author, Business Implementation & Financial Accountability Coach**, helping Christian Female Entrepreneurs break free of the **"Money is a Sin" myth**, manage it wisely, and grow in faith.

We can do all things through Christ who strengthens us. It starts with one step forward, letting God lead the way.

One very important point to consider is that owning a business has always been part of my life from childhood. It's just the challenge of doing something and succeeding at it.

To be successful, you may have to make some extremely hard decisions, but it's up to you to submit your requests before the Lord and allow Him to direct.

As I am writing this book, one verse has come alive in this process, and that is *John chapter 15, verses 1-2, 7: "I am the true vine, and my Father is the husbandman. Every branch in me that beareth not fruit he taketh away; and every branch that beareth fruit, he purgeth it, that it may bring forth more fruit. If ye abide in me, and my words abide in you, ye shall ask what ye will, and it shall be done unto you."*

When we abide in the Lord and remain in His word, He is faithful. He will direct our paths and guide us exactly where we are meant to go.

He can do it alone, but he doesn't want to. He wants a relationship with us.

It is our job, then, to seek wise counsel and get the help and guidance we need. I tried for about a year to just build my business alone. Then, about 12 months later, I had lots of clients but felt overworked and underpaid.

I was not making the amount of money I was accustomed to while employed. I got a call from a potential business coach. He gave me a price of approximately $6000. I was like, "Oh my goodness." I told him to give me two weeks. I considered it, and while I was not financially ready, I stepped out in faith.

Hiring him was the best investment because the next client I took on, I used the pricing method he gave, and wow, just like that, the one customer's fees equaled the total of five.

You see, the coach saw something I didn't. After that client, I learned how to sell the transformation, and that made all the difference in the world.

What I am telling you is, you must be prepared to invest in your business; if not, it just means that you don't believe in your own abilities.

Secondly, as you invest in your business, commit the plans to the Lord. He will bring the right people and clients into your path. He will open those doors that you never even knew existed.

Put James's words to work: **Faith and work working together is priceless.**

Remember, in the book of Isaiah 40:31, it says, ***"But they that wait upon the Lord shall renew their strength; they shall mount up with wings as eagles; they shall run and not be weary; and they shall walk and not faint."***

You have what it takes to achieve a successful business, but you must believe in yourself and embrace the abilities that the Lord has given you.

Let's wrap this up with four simple steps to success using the S.O.A.R acronym:

S - **Seek Opportunities**: God opens doors, but you've got to walk through them. ***"Ask and it will be given to you; seek and you will find; knock and the door will be opened to you."*** *(Matthew 7:7)*

O - **Overcome Obstacles**: Every giant you face is just a stepping stone on your path. ***"I have told you these things, so that in me you may have peace. In this world you will have trouble. But take heart! I have overcome the world."*** *(John 16:33)*

A - **Apply Your Skills**: Use the talents God gave you; they're your tools to build with. ***"Each of you should use whatever gift you have received to serve others, as faithful stewards of God's grace in its various forms."*** *(1 Peter 4:10)*

R - **Rejoice and Repeat**: Celebrate every victory, no matter how small. Then, do it again. *"Rejoice always, pray continually, give thanks in all circumstances; for this is God's will for you in Christ Jesus." (1 Thessalonians 5:16-18)*

Remember, every entrepreneur's journey starts with a dream and a whole lot of faith. Just make sure to keep your piano tuned—you never know when you'll need to play a new tune.

As a Business Implementation and Financial Accountability Coach, I have helped countless businesses achieve business success as we speak, keeping them accountable to being successful and not allowing their business to run them. It is their wealth machine, and to bring it into reality, they must see it that way.

Follow my author page on Amazon for more insights, and don't forget to grab a copy of my workbook for this chapter to start applying these principles today!

Dr. DeShonda Jennings

DJ It Takes A Village LLC
Childcare Coach

https://www.LinkedIn.com/in/deshondajennings
https://www.facebook.com/deshonda.jennings
www.instagram.com/deshonda_j
www.deshondajennings.com
www.10mistakes2avoid.com

Dr. DeShonda Jennings is a dedicated leader in early childhood education, helping families and childcare professionals create thriving environments for children. A devoted mother, Family Childcare Business Owner, Childcare Coach, international speaker, and best-selling author, she brings years of experience to the field. Raised in Kenbridge, VA, her passion for children led her to establish DJ Shining Stars Childcare Program, a successful home-based business serving infants through school-age children. Her program fosters a nurturing space where young learners grow and develop. Beyond childcare, Dr. DeShonda mentors professionals, offering strategies for building sustainable businesses. Through her books and public speaking, she shares practical insights for aspiring providers. Featured on Google Podcasts, CBS, NBC, and The Washington Post, she received the Presidential Lifetime Achievement Award and an Honorary Doctorate in Humanitarianism in 2024. She remains committed to supporting those shaping the future of early childhood education.

From Bankruptcy to Breakthrough:
The L.A.U.N.C.H. to a Legacy

By Dr. DeShonda Jennings

"For unto whomsoever much is given, of him shall be much
required." – Luke 12:48 KJV

Life is a journey with many twists and turns, and sometimes it feels
like the very ground beneath us is shifting. In 2019, I found myself at
one of those life-altering moments. The journey that I thought was
on the path to continued success took a sharp, unexpected detour.
Financial ruin loomed large, and the weight of an uncertain future
threatened to break me. I had spent years building my business, and
I had poured my heart into my family and my community. But now,
I was at the brink of losing it all.

Filing for Chapter 13 bankruptcy was one of the hardest decisions of
my life. It felt like failure. How could I—a woman who had
successfully built a home-based childcare business and coached
countless other entrepreneurs—be facing financial collapse? The
shame and guilt were overwhelming. I felt like I had let everyone
down. My children, my community, my family—all of them had
depended on me, and here I was, fighting to keep my home, my
business, and my dignity intact. But in that moment of despair, I
made a commitment to myself: I would not let this setback define
me. Instead, I would transform it into a breakthrough, a testimony to
resilience, faith, and unwavering determination.

That dark chapter marked the beginning of a new journey—one that
would take me from bankruptcy to breakthrough, from hopelessness
to success, and from financial ruin to a thriving six-figure business.
But none of it happened overnight. It was a journey that required
deep reflection, strategic action, and, most importantly, faith. And

along the way, I created a framework that not only helped me through my recovery but also became the foundation of my business philosophy. This framework is called L.A.U.N.C.H., and it became the roadmap that led me to success.

L: Leverage Your Strengths

When life is difficult, it's easy to focus on what's wrong, to dwell on what we don't have, or to feel as if we've been stripped of everything. But in the midst of financial ruin, I knew that I had something valuable: my skills, experience, and knowledge. I had spent years building a successful Family Childcare Business, and I knew that the expertise I had gained could still be leveraged to create something new.

I had spent countless hours caring for children, understanding their needs, and creating an environment where both children and parents felt supported and nurtured. I had built relationships with families, and I understood the intricacies of running a business that was centered on children's well-being. These were my strengths—skills I could use to rebuild my financial future.

Instead of focusing on the things I didn't have, I decided to focus on what I had to offer. I was in the business of helping others, and that was something I could leverage in this new chapter of my life. The idea of starting over wasn't easy, but by identifying my strengths and leaning into them, I was able to see the opportunities that were still available to me. This was the first step in turning my circumstances around.

A: Assess the Situation

When things seem bleak, it's easy to want to avoid the reality of the situation. But in order to make meaningful progress, I had to take a hard look at where I was. I had to assess everything—my finances, my business, and my personal situation—honestly. This wasn't an easy process, but it was essential.

I sat down with my financial advisor, reviewed all of my debts, and evaluated where my business was financially. I also looked at my personal situation—how much stress I was under, how my family was coping, and what sacrifices had been made in order to keep everything afloat. I had to confront the truth head-on. But this assessment wasn't just about recognizing my shortcomings. It was about identifying the resources I had left—the strengths, the opportunities, and the drive that I could tap into.

During this period, I realized that my business—DJ Shining Stars Childcare—wasn't just a job for me; it was a calling. I knew I had the capacity to create something better, something sustainable, and something that would not only benefit my family but also the families I served. By understanding the full scope of my situation, I was able to set realistic goals for myself. I wasn't just thinking about short-term survival—I was thinking about long-term recovery and growth.

U: Understand the Path Forward

After assessing where I was, the next step was to understand the path forward. In moments of crisis, it's easy to feel lost or overwhelmed by the enormity of the task ahead. But I knew that in order to move forward, I had to educate myself. I sought advice from financial experts, read books, and attended seminars about rebuilding after bankruptcy.

One of the most valuable lessons I learned during this time was that no one could do it alone. I needed help. And so, I reached out to others who had been through similar struggles and had come out the other side. I learned how to negotiate with creditors, how to restructure my business, and how to manage my finances in a way that would set me up for success.

I also took the time to focus on personal development. I realized that my growth as an entrepreneur wasn't just about the technical aspects of running a business—it was about growing my mindset, my resilience, and my capacity to believe in myself again. By understanding the steps needed to move forward, I built a roadmap that would guide me to my breakthrough.

N: Navigate the Challenges

The road to recovery was far from easy. There were days when I felt like giving up, when the obstacles seemed insurmountable, and when I doubted whether I could keep going. But every time I faced a setback, I reminded myself of the commitment I had made to rise above it all.

Each challenge became an opportunity to learn and grow. I encountered moments of doubt and fear, but each one was met with the resolve to push forward. One of the greatest challenges was the emotional toll that bankruptcy took on me. I struggled with feelings of shame, guilt, and fear. But through those emotions, I learned that resilience isn't about avoiding pain—it's about moving forward even when the path isn't clear.

I also learned that challenges don't last forever. Just as seasons change, so do our struggles. By navigating the challenges with persistence and faith, I was able to move past them and keep my eyes on the prize.

C: Commit to Consistency

Consistency is the cornerstone of success. It's easy to get discouraged when things aren't progressing as quickly as you'd like, but I understood that sustainable success requires consistent effort over time. I committed to showing up every day, whether it was working on my finances, improving my business, or simply taking care of myself.

One of the most powerful tools I used was setting small, achievable goals. By focusing on one step at a time, I was able to maintain momentum and stay on track. I also made sure to surround myself with people who supported my journey—family, friends, and mentors who believed in me and reminded me that success was still possible.

It wasn't always easy, and there were many days when I felt like giving up. But I stayed consistent in my actions, and eventually, the results began to show. Through daily effort, I was able to rebuild my business and move closer to my vision of success.

H: Harness the Power of Faith

Throughout this entire process, my faith was the anchor that kept me grounded. When things were uncertain, and when I felt lost, I leaned on my faith. I knew that I wasn't walking this path alone. My faith reminded me that there was a greater plan at work, and that even in the darkest moments, there was light on the other side.

I drew strength from my belief that I was being guided toward something greater than I could imagine. It was through my faith that I found the strength to persevere. It was through my faith that I learned to trust in the process, even when the results weren't immediate. And it was through my faith that I learned to trust myself again.

I believe that faith is a key ingredient in any entrepreneurial journey. Without faith in ourselves and in something greater, it's easy to lose hope. But when we harness the power of faith, we gain the strength to keep going, no matter what obstacles lie ahead.

A Legacy Built Through Resilience

Today, I stand not just as an entrepreneur but as a coach, author, and speaker who is committed to empowering others to achieve their own breakthroughs. The lessons I've learned from my own journey are now the foundation of my work with others. I help fellow childcare providers and aspiring entrepreneurs build sustainable, successful businesses. My story—from bankruptcy to breakthrough—has become a powerful message that inspires others to take action, no matter their circumstances.

One of my proudest accomplishments is receiving the **Presidential Lifetime Achievement Award** in 2024, a recognition that celebrates my contributions to the field of childcare and education. This honor was a testament to the impact I've made in the lives of families and children. It reminded me that even the hardest struggles can lead to the greatest triumphs.

That same year, I was also honored with an **Honorary Doctorate in Humanitarianism**. This recognition solidified my commitment to serving others and empowering those around me to achieve their own greatness. Both of these honors were a reminder that our journeys are not just about our own success—they are about leaving a legacy for others to follow.

The Future of My Legacy

As I reflect on my journey, I am filled with gratitude. What began as a time of personal and financial hardship has turned into a thriving business, a platform for helping others, and a legacy that will continue long after I'm gone. Through it all, I've learned that there is no obstacle too great, no setback too powerful, and no challenge too insurmountable.

Through the L.A.U.N.C.H. framework, I have not only rebuilt my life and business—I've created a legacy. I now share this framework with other entrepreneurs who are facing their own challenges. It is a roadmap for overcoming obstacles, building sustainable businesses, and creating a lasting impact.

As I continue to grow, I am reminded of the words of Luke 12:48: *"For unto whomsoever much is given, of him shall be much required."* This journey has not been easy, but it has been worth every moment. And as I look to the future, I am committed to continuing to serve, inspire, and empower others. My legacy is just beginning, and I am excited to see where it leads.

This is not just my story—it is the story of anyone who has faced hardship, overcome adversity, and emerged stronger on the other side. I encourage you to take your own journey, to rise above your challenges, and to create your own legacy. The breakthrough is waiting for you. Your path to success begins with the first step. Take it.

Nana Adjoa Sifa Amponsah

Founder of Guzakuza

https://www.linkedin.com/in/nana-adjoa-sifa-amponsah-91099950/
www.nadjoasifa.orgwww.guzakuza.com

Nana Adjoa A. Sifa is a gender- lens entrepreneur and ecosystem builder committed to driving change in social investment, agrifood system and amplifying women's voices. As Founder of Guzakuza, she has ignited over 9,000 women across 36 countries, equipping them to build scalable, sustainable businesses through initiatives like Ignite Africa, MentorHer, WiFAI, and SheFarms. A World Economic Forum Global Shaper, UN Women UK Delegate, and NYU-GWSLP Fellow, Nana has shaped global conversations on women, entrepreneurship, and climate. She has spoken on high-level panels, including presenting the Berlin Charter at the G20.Recognised with awards like the UK's Inspiring Women Award and Africa 40 Under 40, her work has been featured in The New York Times, Spore Magazine, and DW TV. She also founded The FeMail, a platform championing women's voices in business. Nana is passionate about unlocking capital, reshaping systems, and creating opportunities for women to thrive in agrifood and beyond.

Don't Build Alone: Find Your Mentor

By Nana Adjoa Sifa Amponsah

I thought I had to do it all myself. The vision, the strategy, the hustle—it felt like a solo mission. In the early days of my entrepreneurial journey, I wore self-reliance like a badge of honor. But behind the scenes, I was navigating storms without a compass, making avoidable mistakes, and silently wishing for someone—anyone—who had walked this road before.

Then I found her.

A mentor. A woman who saw me before the world did. Who challenged my thinking, stretched my comfort zone, and—most importantly—believed in me when I struggled to believe in myself. That relationship didn't just change my business. It changed me.

You don't have to wait for the perfect mentor to appear magically. In this chapter, I'll walk you through how mentorship became my secret weapon—and how you can find, nurture, and grow mentorship relationships that propel you forward. Whether you're building a brand, launching an idea, or scaling your impact, this is your sign: don't build alone. Find your mentor.

The Myth of the Self-Made Woman

There's a seductive story the world loves to tell about women like us.

The story of the self-made woman.

She's fierce. She's focused. She rises before dawn and builds her empire with nothing but grit, guts, and a laptop. She never cries, never doubts, and certainly never asks for help. She is her own blueprint, her own boardroom, her own safety net.

And while that version makes for a great headline, it leaves out the truth: most women who build anything of substance do not build it alone.

I believed the myth once. In fact, I lived it.

In my early years as a founder, I carried the weight of every decision, every vision, every failed pitch like a badge of honour. I was trying to prove—to myself and to the world—that I could figure it out. That I didn't need a handout. That I was enough.

But what I didn't realise then was that independence without support isn't strength—it's isolation.

And isolation is where dreams quietly wither.

It's where second-guessing becomes a lifestyle.

It's where brilliance burns out before it ever lights the world.

It took hitting an emotional wall to realise that I wasn't meant to walk this path alone. That the most successful women I admired had advisors, coaches, sponsors—mentors—behind the scenes, holding space for them, sharpening their ideas, opening doors they didn't even know existed.

It's one woman whispering to another: "You don't have to do this the hard way."

And if you're reading this, nodding along because you've felt that same lonely stretch of the road—this chapter is for you. Not just to inspire you, but to equip you. To remind you that asking for guidance is not a detour; it is part of the path. In fact, it's the most direct route to legacy.

Because here's the truth:

You can build alone.

But you will build better when you don't.

The Power of Being Seen

Before you take your first big leap in entrepreneurship, before you even call yourself a founder, there is often one quiet but life-altering moment:

Someone sees something in you before you fully see it in yourself.

For me, that moment came in a dusty meeting room, somewhere between frustration and fatigue. I had pitched yet another bold vision for women in agribusiness. I was met with polite nods and the usual skepticism—until one person pulled me aside and said, "You're not crazy. You're early. And you're necessary."

That sentence didn't give me funding. It didn't hand me a business plan. But it gave me something far more valuable: permission. Permission to trust my voice. Permission to move forward even when the applause hadn't yet started. Permission to take up space.

That person became one of my first informal mentors. He didn't promise me weekly check-ins or long-term commitments. What he offered was belief—and sometimes, belief is the very oxygen your vision needs to breathe again.

Mentorship is not always formal. Sometimes it shows up as:

- A well-timed email after a tough rejection.
- A seat at a table you didn't think you deserved.
- A name dropped in a room full of decision-makers.
- Or simply, someone saying, "You've got this. Keep going."

The world teaches us to seek visibility—to post, pitch, and perform. But the first kind of visibility that matters is the kind that happens in private: when someone looks beyond your résumé and sees your potential.

That is the power of being seen.

And once you experience it, you realise it's not something to hoard.

It's something to pass on.

Because when you truly see someone, and you tell her what you see—she begins to see it too.

That's how confidence grows. That's how communities rise. That's how ecosystems shift—from the inside out.

So if you're waiting for permission to rise, let this be it:

You are not asking for too much. You are stepping into what's already yours.

What Makes a Great Mentor (and What Doesn't)

After years of being mentored—and mentoring others—I've learned this:

A great mentor doesn't just give answers. She expands your thinking.

Not every person with experience should be your mentor. And not every successful person will be good for your journey. Mentorship, when done well, is more than wisdom-sharing—it's a relationship rooted in alignment, trust, and mutual respect.

So what exactly should you look for?

Three Types of Mentors Every Entrepreneur Needs:

1. The Guide

This mentor has walked the road you're on. She knows the pitfalls, shortcuts, and long game.

She'll challenge your strategy, ask you uncomfortable questions, and show you how to think—not what to think.

You need her for her mind.

"Have you considered another model?"

"Tell me how this solves the root problem."

"You're playing small here."

2. The Mirror

This one sees the you behind the pitch deck. She reflects your fears, patterns, and limiting beliefs back to you—not to judge, but to help you grow.

You need her for your soul.

"Why are you hesitating?"

"What story are you telling yourself about failure?"

"You don't need to shrink to be accepted."

3. The Door Opener

This mentor has access to rooms you haven't yet entered—and isn't afraid to say your name when opportunity knocks.

She sponsors you, advocates for you, and helps you build social capital.

You need her for her network.

"You need to meet this investor."

"I'll introduce you to the programme director."

"Here's how you position yourself in that space."

Sometimes one person holds all three roles. Most times, they don't—and that's okay.

Your mentorship circle should be as dynamic as your dreams.

Red Flags to Watch For:

- They talk more than they listen. True mentorship involves curiosity, not lectures.
- They center themselves. If every conversation ends with their story, not yours, take note.
- They undermine your voice. A mentor should sharpen your vision, not replace it.
- They are unavailable or inconsistent. Time is valuable. A great mentor honours yours and their own.

A Truth Worth Holding:

The best mentors aren't always the most visible. They're the most intentional.

It's better to have one committed, aligned mentor than ten impressive names who never truly invest in you.

And sometimes, your mentor is not in your industry—but shares your values.

Sometimes she's not ten steps ahead—just two.

And that's enough.

The goal is not to collect mentors.

The goal is to connect deeply with a few who truly get you—and stretch you.

How to Find the Right Mentor (Even If You Don't Know Where to Start): The Practical Guide

One of the questions I hear most from early-stage founders is:

"But how do I actually find a mentor?"

It's a fair question. We often imagine mentors as these unreachable legends we need to "earn access" to—when in truth, mentorship can be found and fostered in unexpected places, It is for the intentional. You don't need a viral business or a fancy title—you need clarity, courage, and consistency.

Here's how to start:

Step 1: Get Clear on What You Need

Before you look for a mentor, take stock of what you truly need right now—not in five years, but today. Take a moment to reflect:

- Where am I stuck?
- What do I want to grow in?
- Do I need mindset support, business advice, or strategic introductions?
- Am I looking for help with my business model or strategy?
- Do I need someone to hold me accountable and build my confidence?
- Are you looking for connections and access to new networks?

Knowing your "why" helps you attract the right kind of mentor—not just someone impressive on paper.

The more specific you are, the more aligned your mentor search becomes.

Step 2: Look Around, Not Just Up

We often think mentors have to be super successful CEOs or famous founders. But truthfully, some of the best mentors are just a few steps ahead of you.

- Is there someone in your community, WhatsApp group, or LinkedIn network whose work you admire?
- Is there a fellow alum from a program you've been part of who is thriving in your industry?

Don't overlook peer mentors—they're often the most accessible and relatable.

Step 3: Show Up Where They Are

Mentors don't appear out of thin air. They show up in the rooms you're consistent in.

Visibility builds connection. Show up consistently and authentically.

Where to Look for Mentors:

Within Your Existing Circles That person who's always giving thoughtful feedback in your group chats? That peer a few steps ahead in your industry? Mentorship doesn't always come from above—it can come alongside.

At Events You Already Attend Attend industry events, workshops, fellowships, or webinars, pitch competitions, accelerators, panels—these are goldmines. Don't just attend. Approach. Follow up. Ask meaningful questions, and build real connections.

Online Communities Join online communities in your niche (e.g. agribusiness, tech, health, creative industries). LinkedIn, founder forums, mastermind groups—digital proximity is powerful. Comment, engage, and be brave enough to send the DM.

Through Warm Introductions Be bold and ask someone you trust: "Is there someone in your network who'd be open to a short conversation? I'm navigating [Write your specific need], and I'd value their insight."

Reverse Mentorship Yes—you may have something to offer, too. Your unique lens, energy, or digital savvy may be just what a senior leader needs. Mutually beneficial mentorship is a rising model—and it works.

Step 4: Reach Out With Intention

Your message doesn't need to be perfect—it just needs to be real. Don't ask "Will you be my mentor?" right away. Instead, start with curiosity and respect. Here's how:

Sample Message (Short & Sincere):

Hi Nana,

I've been following your work on Agribusiness, and it really resonates with where I'm trying to go with my journey in [brief mention of your focus]. I admire how you [something specific—authenticity matters].

I'm in the early stages of [your business/project], and I'd love to learn from your experience—if you're open to a 15–20 minute conversation. I truly believe a single conversation with someone like you could make a big difference.

Thanks for considering this, and whether or not it's possible, I appreciate the inspiration you share.

Warm regards,

[Your Name]

Step 5: Add Value Before You Ask for It

Even if you're new, you can give. That might be by:

- Sharing their work online
- Offering to volunteer at their event
- Giving feedback or testimonials
- Simply being a thoughtful, consistent presence in their community

Value builds trust. Start by being a learner and a contributor.

Bonus Tip: Turn "No" Into "Not Yet"

If someone doesn't respond or says no, don't take it personally. Follow them, stay engaged with their work, and keep the door open. Timing matters.

The mentor you're looking for might already be watching you— waiting to see if you'll take that first brave step. So go ahead. Be intentional, be open, and remember: you don't have to build alone.

Becoming the Mentor You Wish You Had

Every time I speak to a room of founders, I remind them of this truth:

You are someone else's answered prayer.

Not someday—today.

We often look for mentors without realizing we've already become one in someone else's story. The questions you've answered. The time you've given. The encouragement you offered when someone was ready to quit. That is mentorship.

Yes, you may still be building. Yes, you may still feel unsure.

But here's the secret seasoned entrepreneurs rarely say out loud:

Mentorship isn't about having it all figured out. It's about showing up with honesty, humility, and heart.

So how do you become the mentor you once searched for?

Start Where You Are

You don't need a formal title. Offer to review a pitch deck. Recommend a tool. Make an introduction. Share your story—not the polished version, but the real one.

Sometimes the most powerful thing you can say is:

"I've been there too. Here's what helped me."

Create Safe Spaces

Founders—especially women—need rooms where vulnerability is welcomed, not judged. Be the kind of mentor who listens deeply, speaks truth gently, and cheers wildly.

Pay It Forward with Purpose

When you rise, lift others. When you learn, teach.

The mentorship you received? Pass it on.

One of the greatest legacies we can leave as entrepreneurs is not just a successful business, but a generation we've empowered through our wisdom, wounds, and wins.

Sustaining Mentorship Relationships

Finding a mentor is just the beginning. Like any valuable relationship, mentorship needs tending.

Great mentorship isn't one-sided. It's not just about receiving—it's about engaging, respecting, and showing up. If you want to keep the relationship thriving, here's how:

Stay Consistent

Schedule periodic check-ins. Even a quarterly message saying, "Here's what's changed and where I could use your insight" keeps the connection alive.

Be Coachable

Apply the advice. Reflect on it. Then come back and share results. Mentors want to see growth—they're not investing in your perfection, but your progress.

Show Appreciation

A simple "thank you" or sharing a win they contributed to goes a long way. Tag them in your journey when appropriate. Everyone likes to feel their time mattered.

Keep it Mutual

Share an article they'd enjoy. Introduce them to someone relevant. You may not have their experience yet—but you have value to give. Offer it.

The best mentees are those who evolve into peers—then into partners.

That's the long game of mentorship.

The Ripple Effect: What Happens When Women Mentor Women

There is something uniquely powerful about women mentoring women—especially in entrepreneurship.

We speak not just from strategy, but from survival.

We share not just tools, but truths.

And we carry the weight of not just our dreams—but the ones we've been told are "too much."

When a woman entrepreneur reaches back and uplifts another, it's not charity—it's legacy.

Here's what happens when we mentor each other:

- Businesses grow faster—and last longer.
- Confidence replaces confusion.
- Gatekeeping turns into hand-holding.

- Networks widen, voices rise, and glass ceilings start to crack—louder.

Every time you mentor another woman, you change the ecosystem.

You show what's possible. You give permission. You rewrite the script.

And in doing so, you don't just light her path.

You illuminate your own.

You Are Not Alone. You Were Never Meant to Be.

In the unpredictable journey of entrepreneurship, there will be seasons of doubt, delay, and deep questioning. But mentorship reminds us that we are not navigating this terrain alone.

Someone has walked this path before you—and someone is watching you walk it now.

So reach out. Ask boldly. Receive humbly. And when your turn comes, give generously.

Because this is how we rise. Not in isolation, but in intention.

Don't build alone. Find your mentor. Be one. And watch the ripple begin.

Erica Elliott

WarriorHeart Healing Hearts, LLC
Coach, Counselor, Speaker, Author, Consultant

https://linktr.ee/WarriorHeartxo
https://www.facebook.com/warriorheartxo
https://www.instagram.com/warriorheartxo
https://msha.ke/warriorheartxo
https://www.linkedin.com/in/erica-elliott-ms-lpc-b90911150

I possess a Master's Degree in Counseling Psychology and have invested over three decades in my career as a Licensed Counselor, Certified Brain Health Coach, and Certified Health Integrative Medicine Professional. My expertise encompasses a broad spectrum of therapeutic approaches, such as Neurobiology, ADHD and Neurodiversity, Somatic Therapy, Energy Medicine, NLP, CBT, RET, EFT, TFT, Theology, EMDR, the Gottman Method, alongside Mindfulness and Meditation. I am an author and spent over a decade in the military. I am the owner of WarriorHeart Healing Hearts where I champion a comprehensive healing philosophy that harmonizes the mind, body, and spirit. I help individuals clear up the mess to discover their MASTERPIECE using a combination of healing modalities to rapidly rewire for success! Throughout my career, I've had the privilege of helping thousands of individuals, viewing my work not merely as a profession but as a calling. I am truly passionate about empowering others to grow, heal, and soar, unlocking the incredible life that God has always envisioned for them. Having navigated my own share of trials, traumas, and triggers, I deeply understand that healing flourishes through compassionate relationships. Together, we cultivate resilience and vitality, transforming legacies. Like iron sharpening iron, if you're looking for support or just want to connect, you were destined for greatness! Be Blessed and Be a Blessing!

Embracing the Leap of Faith

By Erica Elliott

Have you ever had a dream where you imagined something beautiful, magical, and exciting, but it felt as if you were standing on the outside of a glass peering in, watching all the people as they were performing these magical feats, and you weren't allowed to enter? You watched as others executed these remarkable feats while you were left outside, wondering if there's a concealed entrance you'd overlooked. Those around you appear to know precisely what actions to take, where to head, and how to bring their aspirations to life. You can't shake the feeling that you're missing a vital element, though it remains just out of reach.

When I contemplate my experience with imposter syndrome, this is what it felt like for me. In different situations, this sensation can morph into feelings of fear or anxiety, as if you're perpetually concerned that others might discover your lack of knowledge or realize you aren't as capable as you believe you ought to be. It's so interesting to me how our minds work and what it takes to get out of our own way sometimes. Though everyone will face limiting beliefs from time to time and have to work through them, imposter syndrome is like a distortion in the brain similar to body dysmorphia. Where reality and thoughts don't match. Some of the areas I have struggled with and overcome are areas I have had high achievements, success, or even awards. I was also told by lots of people how good or even great I was in a particular area, but it felt in my brain that they were just saying that to be nice. Some of these areas I worked through more easily than others. What I often found was that I would spend lots of money and countless hours of training, trying to make sure I was truly worthy, and even then, sometimes struggled in an almost paralyzing fashion.

To succeed in anything in life, you have to make a choice to try and do things you've never done before. Taking a leap into the unknown is essential for growth and transformation. As humans, we often find solace in the familiar, crafting mental safe havens that shield us from the uncertainties in life. It's interesting to explore how our minds operate. You may feel accomplished in certain areas of life while grappling with insecurities in others. This dichotomy has been a significant part of my journey, as I yearned to step into a space that felt both exciting and forbidden, accompanied by the heavy weight of imposter syndrome.

Here is a deeper dive into imposter syndrome. Imposter syndrome is a psychological phenomenon where individuals doubt their abilities and fear being exposed as a fraud, despite clear evidence of their skills and accomplishments. Those experiencing this syndrome often believe they do not deserve their success and attribute their achievements to luck or other external factors rather than their own efforts.

Several factors can contribute to the development of imposter syndrome:

Perfectionism: Individuals who set excessively high standards for themselves may feel inadequate when they fail to meet those expectations. Perfectionism can come from a place of feeling like you need to be perfect to be loved, accepted, or worthy. Unfortunately, no one reaches perfection, and it takes a toll on our psyche. There are days that we don't measure up, and it doesn't make us bad; it makes us human.

Background Influences: Growing up in environments that prioritize achievement can lead to internalized feelings of not being good enough. Sometimes, we learn that that is the only time we are celebrated, which can be a huge dopamine surge and lead us to needing or craving more.

Social Comparisons: Regularly comparing oneself to others, especially in competitive situations, can intensify feelings of inadequacy. We can be trained by our family or society to compare ourselves to others, which can create us often trying to figure out a path that looks like theirs instead of sinking into our own unique badass masterpiece.

Cultural Norms: Societal pressures can play a role, particularly for women and minorities in fields where they are underrepresented. Being in the military back in the 90s, with less than 10% of women in the Army, made this an issue because we were often trying to compete with males.

New Experiences: Taking on new responsibilities or entering unfamiliar situations can trigger feelings of being an imposter. For many people, experiencing new things is fun and exciting, but for those with imposter syndrome, it can feel like getting a tooth pulled without anesthesia.

If you or someone you know struggles with this, here are some tips to work through it. Also, always know you are not alone, and delving deeper to heal with a counselor or coach can be so helpful. To overcome imposter syndrome, consider the following steps:

Acknowledge Your Feelings: Recognize and accept that these feelings are common and do not reflect your true abilities. When we learn to tune in and allow ourselves to feel a feeling and even call it by name, we can release it more easily in the brain and body.

Reframe Negative Thoughts: Challenge negative beliefs about yourself and replace them with positive affirmations of your skills and accomplishments. Everyone has strengths and skills, and it's important for us to regularly acknowledge them, or we are constantly looking outside of ourselves to be affirmed.

Share Your Feelings: Talk to trusted friends, mentors, or colleagues about your experiences. Sharing can help normalize your feelings and provide support. Sometimes, just having a place to share is a powerful release. Many people don't want to overshare or may not have people they can share with, but you can always get a coach or counselor to help you process.

Celebrate Achievements: Keep a record of your successes and reflect on them regularly to reinforce your sense of accomplishment. This is one I find when clients begin to do this, they remember accomplishments they forgot and find new inspiration inside.

Seek Professional Help: If feelings of inadequacy persist, consider speaking with a mental health professional or life coach who can provide guidance and strategies to cope. Remember, you don't have to do this alone. Jesus had disciples he did life with. The disciples were sent out in twos. Throughout the Bible, it shows that having another human healthy connection is important.

By taking these steps, individuals can work toward a healthier self-perception and build confidence in their abilities. I myself saw a coach to clear the unconscious stuck and cluttered beliefs.

In my quest to follow my true calling, I frequently found myself torn between my aspirations and the shadows of my fears. Since my childhood, I have poured my creativity into writing, crafting everything from short stories, songs, and poetry. My desire to express myself and share my journey was often eclipsed by an overwhelming sense of inadequacy. After spending over three decades as a counselor, I had absorbed the lesson that personal sharing could blur professional boundaries, making me apprehensive about revealing anything that might cast others in a negative light or trigger people to remember their own negative past.

However, as I reflected on my past, I recognized that my experiences could serve as a beacon for others. The dynamics within my family had evolved, presenting opportunities for growth that I could share. Still, the insidious grip of imposter syndrome held me back, filling my mind with self-doubt, even though I held a master's degree and had received praise from professors for my writing skills.

To illustrate the extent of my struggle, I recall the research thesis I undertook for my Master's in Counseling Psychology. I selected an underexplored topic, investigating the interplay between quality of life and the balance of happiness versus depression. Through persistent effort, I gathered 240 assessments from the geriatric population I served, a feat my professor deemed exceptional and vital for publication. Out of 26 students in my accelerated program, only six of us graduated on time, successfully navigating the demanding thesis approval process. I was among those six, encouraged to publish my findings due to their merit. Yet, instead of seizing the opportunity, I hesitated, crippled by the fear that my achievement would not be seen worthy by publishing committee.

This encapsulates the debilitating nature of imposter syndrome. Despite dedicating countless hours to my education and striving to prove my worth, I often felt inadequate. I convinced myself that only after reaching certain academic milestones would I finally be ready to showcase my writing. Driven by this belief, I applied to pursue a doctorate program in the summer of 2020, eagerly anticipating a new beginning in January 2021. The thought thrilled me, as I had always longed to earn my doctorate. However, life had its own surprises, and God had other plans for me.

A severe health crisis struck in November of 2020 after having COVID and not resting, which left me grappling with adrenal fatigue, autoimmune issues, chronic fatigue syndrome, myalgia, post-COVID syndrome, and a brain injury. I had word-finding and memory problems. I felt like my life was over in so many ways, and I wondered if I could even get my life back. The struggle was so intense. I remember crying out to God, wondering how I could live like this. I could barely walk to the kitchen, my body felt like it would never be the same, and the depression and anxiety would overtake me at times. It was during this time that God gently let me know He was there for me, and I would need to do the things I taught so many who struggled with autoimmune issues, chronic illness, and brain injuries. This really wasn't reassuring at the time. It felt more daunting than hopeful, but as a mom, I knew I needed to show the same strength I had when my daughter went through her debilitating illness and almost died. As God brought her to my mind and what she and I went through to get her to the amazing place she is today, I felt a remembrance of God's faithfulness. It was a hard road ahead, like walking up a mountain with a 200-pound weight on my back. My brain often felt like it was on fire, with relentless migraines from hell. Some days only a few inches forward, some days a few feet, and other days it felt as though I slid down the hill only to start over again.

As I embarked on my journey of healing, an undeniable tug on my heart beckoned me from God, urging me to write a book that had long simmered within, nurtured by His persistent whispers. This time, the call was more insistent. Initially, I found myself resisting, much like Jonah, attempting to flee from my divine assignment. Yet, the gentle nudges from within became a force I could no longer ignore.

Caught in a tug-of-war, I wrestled with my thoughts. The subject matter of the book danced on the edge of controversy within certain circles of Christianity, and I feared misrepresenting the profound lessons God had imparted to me. Moreover, I questioned my own abilities ... who was I to undertake such a task without the accolades of a doctorate?

But as I reflect on the journey of writing and publishing, I recognize that precisely because I lacked those credentials, I was called to write now. It was never about the accolades or the knowledge I possessed; it was about surrendering to the process and allowing God to shine through my vulnerability. I am grateful for the healing from imposter syndrome, which has empowered me to write with authenticity. This journey has not only allowed me to share my story but has also opened doors to reach and uplift others around the world. It is my deepest desire to help set others free from the mess within, discovering their MASTERPIECE.

With a mix of fear and faith, I began to write my story. I still did my homework, going through the courses on how to publish a book and such. I also interviewed people who had manifested blessings on my YouTube channel (you can find it connected on my website) to help ensure I was on the right track. I prayed fervently for guidance, asking God to lead me to those whom I could connect with. Then, I came upon She Rises Studios. I vividly remember my first coffee chat with Hanna; her genuine compassion and commitment to uplifting women resonated deeply with me. It was clear that her mission transcended business; she was dedicated to helping women share their stories and inspire others.

As I continued to weave my narrative, December 2024 marked a significant milestone in my life—I published my first book, *Breath of Heaven: Manifesting God's Way*. In this work, I guide readers on a transformative journey, revealing how God has taught me to manifest blessings through biblical principles intertwined with brain science and clear the mess blocking our blessings in life. I offer actionable steps, using scripture and neuropsychological tools to help rewire minds for success and abundance, demonstrating that faith and science are in harmony.

Additionally, I was honored to contribute to the anthology *Her Healthy Glow: Embrace Wellness and Radiate Confidence from the Inside Out*, which achieved USA bestseller status in four categories. Writing had always been a dream of mine. Yet, I constantly battled self-doubt, questioning whether I was truly capable. Despite holding a master's degree in counseling psychology and over 30 years of experience in the field, I still felt the heavy grip of imposter syndrome—a common struggle for many, especially those with ADD. Even when I received honors, the effort often felt minimized inside. Today, I am free! Free to be me! Free to live my dreams and purpose, and you can be, too!

The reality is, no matter how well you perform, your mind can be shackled by limiting beliefs that hinder blessings. As I dismantled these mental barriers, blessings began to continuously flow, with at least ten books within this next year. I am immensely grateful for God's guidance and love as I stepped into uncharted territory and now am living my dream and purpose—helping people heal and clear the mess to discover their Masterpiece in another thrilling way through writing. What joy fills my soul as I think of the impact of helping others grow. I am so grateful to God.

The blessings that have unfolded from this journey are amazing, and the connections I've forged with other women on similar paths have been life-changing. If you find yourself wrestling with similar challenges, I encourage you to confront those blocks and take the leap of faith. Ask God for guidance and follow your heart. The rewards on the other side are beyond what you can imagine.

Remember, you are not alone, and the transformation you seek is within reach. Let's embark on this journey together—your masterpiece awaits, guided by faith and the promise of a brighter future. As a brain health coach, I help people clear the mess to discover their Masterpiece! Imagine soaring in your life's purpose and abundance as you dive deep in my Masterpiece God Centered Mastery Coaching Course using the 777 Method God gave me to clearly soar in life. Be Blessed and be a Blessing!

Ardenna Downing

Founder of Callery Counseling PLLC

https://www.linkedin.com/in/ardenna-downing-41781b94/
https://www.facebook.com/profile.php?id=61569274140068
https://www.instagram.com/callery_counseling
www.callerycounseling.com
https://ardennadowning.substack.com/

Ardenna Downing is a Licensed Professional Clinical Counselor in California and Texas and has been a mental health therapist for approximately 15 years. She is an EMDR certified and Brainspotting therapist whose career has spanned from working in one of the largest family justice centers in the world to mobile crisis outreach and victim's services for police. Ardenna's passion is working with trauma in groups and has experience in the following settings: jail, hospital, shelters, and outreach centers. Ardenna is an advocate for healing through somatic and creative expression including writing, drawing, painting, and sand tray. One of her favorite forms of creative expression is writing. She is an author and has been published in various magazines centering life experiences and mental health reflection. She is also the author of a 40 day journal for those in their forties entitled "Forty for Forties: Transform and Reflect on your Life's Journey."

First Generation Everything

By Ardenna Downing

I am "first generation everything," as I'd like to call it. Most of my life, I have worked on "figuring it out" in order to survive, manage, and thrive. I was raised to live a conventional life. As a young Black girl raised in a Baptist church in the south, obedience was expected. There were many restrictions, but I also observed people with degrees and career paths I hadn't heard of, which planted seeds of possibility in my young mind. A step in entrepreneurship starts with seeing what you want to be in other people, even if you aren't there just yet.

Neither of my parents nor grandparents, to my knowledge, were entrepreneurs or completed college; my father had made an attempt at higher education but didn't graduate. I had no blueprint for college or being an entrepreneur.

I was raised primarily by my maternal grandparents until the age of 9, when my grandfather passed away. Education was important to my grandmother, and she made sure that I had as much as I needed to be successful. She would do things like driving me and my brother to the next city over for better library access. The lesson here is that sometimes you have to literally and figuratively go the distance to get what's better for you, as opposed to resources that are conveniently nearby. While my grandmother's efforts were great, she couldn't fully prepare me for college. I remember her having opened a savings account that only had about $1,500 for college. That was it. We didn't know how much it took, but God always provided.

These were the financial obstacles, but the mental and emotional obstacles were greater. At the beginning of my senior year of high school, my mother died exactly one week before my 17th birthday. We had to bury her the day before. My beloved grandmother, who raised me, died a year later. I had lost two mother figures by the time I was 18 years old.

These events, unbeknownst to me at the time, spearheaded me into risk-taking and adapting to change rapidly, anticipating challenge and response. When my mother died, I had an attitude of not caring what people thought, at least temporarily, because nothing mattered as she was gone. I learned early on that life can be cruel and change fast, and you have to learn how to ride the waves or be snuffed out. By experiencing unexpected grief, I learned to fearlessly take care of my wants and needs and approach life with a very flexible and daring attitude.

I have maintained this approach ever since then. It is still not comfortable, but it is the only way I have learned how to live, which is an advantage as an entrepreneur.

When my grandmother died, I was a first-semester college student. By this time, "sink or swim" had been reinforced. No one was going to save me, including paying my bills. So, I did what needed to be done to survive. I had some support from my family, but it wasn't enough to pay tuition or be able to live on my own. I also realized that despite being an "independent woman," I have consistently reached out and have asked for help when needed. It has not always been comfortable, but it is necessary in order to have the energy, stamina, and wisdom to be a successful entrepreneur.

When safety isn't present, your mind begins to set you up for success, which, if you aren't careful, can turn into an overwhelming amount of anxiety, perfectionism, and other challenges that arise when you feel as if you have no control. My mind did this, I believe, because I was primed for it. If my early life had been set up differently, I may have failed and given up. My college's motto is "Ut Prosim," which is Latin for "That I May Serve." I took this to heart and eventually became a mental health therapist.

I thought that college was hard, but graduate school was harder for me personally. While I experienced a lot of hardship and pain, I was not, at least in my opinion, a true entrepreneur. I had the grit for it, but still only had the same mindset of completing school and finding a job.

I do not regret my experiences, as they have refined me and provided me with the education and experience to be successful as an individual. But I had also learned that who I am would never be fully self-actualized working under someone else's plan.

I am a free spirit, and the way I lived wasn't allowing me to experience freedom. I had security in my work, but no true freedom. As some would say, freedom is not free. After being a public servant in a variety of positions in the mental health world for over 10 years, my student loans were forgiven in 2023. I no longer had to work certain jobs in order to meet a requirement. I am still adjusting to this reality, because freedom, while good, is also an adjustment. Providing myself grace and flexibility in learning who I am without the security of working for someone else has been key.

There may be some grief with forging your own path. Your mindset will need to change in many ways. Thinking of oneself as an "entity" instead of an "employee" can be a very hard adjustment, but it is doable. When you believe that you "are the thing" as opposed to being "a part of the thing," then you are able to shift into a place of ownership of self as a creator.

Once I moved to California and passed my licensure exam requirement to be a practicing therapist, I looked for work and interviewed for multiple organizations. I was even offered employment on multiple occasions, but what they wanted from me didn't sit right with my spirit. I noticed the same sense of weariness and dread creep up within my mind and body in anticipating how to fulfill the unrealistic needs and wants of corporations. I didn't want to compromise myself anymore.

Before I quit my last full-time job in December 2023, I had developed an LLC in October 2019. At the time, I had infrequent clientele while working a full-time job. I positioned myself to do this by seeking out other business owners, reading literature, and signing up for non-profit business assistance such as S.C.O.R.E. At some point in time, I gained enough knowledge and courage from these efforts, which led to a crossroads within myself. I had to decide which risk I was willing to take: the potential financial instability of being on my own and free, or being unfulfilled and drained with a stable job.

You may have to ask yourself this question as well, but the thing is, money can always be made. Your sanity may come at a more permanent cost. This reminds me of a line in the movie *Willy Wonka & the Chocolate Factory*: Grandpa George says, "There's plenty of money out there. They print more every day. But this ticket, there are only five of them in the whole world, and that's all there's ever going to be. Only a dummy would give this up for something as common as money." Your golden ticket is your business; it is a freedom with unlimited opportunity and potential.

Self-employment can come with challenges such as expensive healthcare that may be subpar to what you are provided for when working for someone else, paying an exorbitant amount of taxes, along with being penalized and even sued, where even your personal assets can be taken if you don't structure your business appropriately.

The best thing to do, in my opinion and from experience, is to observe others run a business and read about considerations to be a successful business owner. Obtain as much knowledge as possible about what to do and not do, and be comfortable with the consequences of your decisions, shake it off, and pivot.

I mentioned earlier how you are the "entity" as opposed to being an employee. But it is important to remember that this needs to be flexible as well. Grey area matters. While you are the face of the business and brand, you will at times have to separate your personal self from the life of your business. For instance, I have social media accounts for my personal and professional life, and when I am on my business page, I have to remind myself that I am not liking posts or responding to people as an individual; I am running the page as my professional self. There is a balance to this as well because you don't want to be so separate from who you are as a professional entity and your authentic self that people don't get a sense of what to make of you.

I'd like to visit a metaphor via a story about something that recently happened to me. I was engaging in a virtual training to enhance my practice. During one of my breaks on day two, I went outside to get fresh air. I was walking around and noticed that there was a snake on a tree stump, something that wasn't there the day before. I was about 6 feet away and noticed that I didn't feel fear, yet I was curious, wanting to know if it was a) real, b) a threat, and c) a situation that I needed to act on if it was real. There was no panic, just surprise.

Whether it was a perceived threat or not, my mind kind of interpreted it as one. Despite the fact that the situation may not actually have harmed me, I approached it as if it potentially could. I chose to investigate from a distance by observing and considering what I already knew about snakes being cold-blooded reptiles. It took some time, but I finally determined that the snake was not real. I waited and checked on it again later, and it was in the same spot, but I was still cautious. So, what can we take from this situation in the name of entrepreneurship?

Imagine that this snake is your business, and your responses to it are how you decide to treat and manage it. When you first come across the vision of this business, what do you notice about yourself and how you perceive it? What feelings arise? How should you approach it? Do you need to take a moment to step away, come back to reanalyze how you want to approach it? What beliefs and ideas do you already have about the business that can provide insight into present circumstances? Are you the same person when experiencing a real threat versus a perceived one, as it pertains to your business? Would you approach the circumstances the same?

How my mind chose to approach the snake situation is a perfect example of how I naturally approach life circumstances, both personal and professional. I didn't know that analyzing like this was a strength until I became an adult.

I took the Gallup StrengthsFinder assessment through an employer in my mid-twenties, and they held a team-building day, processing all of our top five traits.

My top five were all in the Strategic Thinking domain. The company I worked for had between 150 and 200 people, and I noticed that the majority of people had a mix of all of the domains. I was one of a handful of people who scored in one area across the board in the top 5, which is rare. I discovered a superpower in my mid-twenties: strategy!

For me, taking assessments has been helpful in discovering who I am as an entrepreneur. I recommend the Strong Interest Inventory, Gallup StrengthsFinder, the Holland Interest Inventory, and Myers-Briggs Type Inventory as good places to start. I took these four assessments over a span of years, and they helped me to better understand my skill areas, interests, strengths, and consistent parts of me. Understanding who you are helps you to understand your business.

My strength in strategy has never been fail-proof. As an entrepreneur, you must recalculate and be flexible in order to pivot when circumstances don't pan out. If not, you may find yourself stuck in the problem instead of forgiving yourself, processing the feelings around the failure, and moving forward differently.

We will fail at times and experience setbacks, but our interpretation of the failure and what we should do about it is very important. You can grieve, experience a variety of thoughts, and also need to make space for some action. Courage often appears in these circumstances as an entrepreneur because you may have to adjust to your fear and anxiety in order to forge ahead.

I have had to sit with a lot of feelings about my approach to business. Sometimes, a misconception is that feelings aren't important and that in order to run a successful business, you have to "suck it up." But our feelings give us insight and signal to us our strengths, weaknesses, thoughts, and actions. The nature of my business is somewhat centered around feelings, so understanding and experiencing them are important for my survival and success as an entrepreneur.

James Clear wrote a book called *Atomic Habits* in which he says that "You don't rise to the levels of your goals, you fall to the levels of your systems." Essentially, you can have goals and visions as an entrepreneur, but what are the workable steps that you will need in place to get there? Do you have a workable system for marketing, networking, payments, developing a product, etc?

Being a business owner has at times been scary. While I own a private practice, I have needed to be flexible and obtain contractor work to supplement times when I didn't have enough clientele. I recently "weaned" myself out of a relationship with a company that credentialed me for insurance and provided referrals, as I want more freedom in how my business is structured. Business dynamics change and are to be expected. Growing pains are inevitable.

I write down what people say to me sometimes to give me added strength and reminders of myself when I am vulnerable and experience some self-doubt and anxiety about expanding my business. I am also still learning the culture of California and am still working on building my networking needs. Reputation and network are important parts of entrepreneurship, and if you have neither, then the likelihood of success will only go so far.

My accomplishments include being featured in media such as newspapers and podcasts, being published multiple times, and successfully negotiating and developing U.S. and international business relationships and work. I am financially stable, enjoy my freedom to work the way I want to, and have good retention of clientele. I am currently developing and have been booked for workshops on mental health topics that integrate expressive arts, which has always been a healing medium for me. By doing what I want to do with my skill set and interests, I am more satisfied with my career path, therefore, more fulfilled.

My life would not be on the trajectory it is now if I had stayed put as a conventional thinker. I am finally prioritizing what is best for myself, and this journey has been worth it a thousand times over.

Nytisha Davis

Founder and CEO of Phillips Mobile Labs LLC

www.linkedin.com/in/nytisha-davis-8b7612198
https://www.facebook.com/phillipsmobilelabs
https://www.instagram.com/phillipsmobilelabs
www.Phillipsmobilelabs.com
https://www.aliveshoes.com/natash-3
https://www.aliveshoes.com/natash-10

My name is Nytisha Davis, and I am the founder and CEO of Phillips Mobile Labs LLC, where we develop and create mobile lab solutions. I am also the creative designer behind Na'Tash shoes, a brand that combines style and comfort for women. Additionally, I co-authored the inspiring book "She Stands Strong," which showcases the resilience of women. Originally from Pennsylvania, I now live in the beautiful state of Arizona with my husband, where I continue to pursue my passion for empowering others. I am a proud mother of three adult children and a dedicated grandmother to five lovely grandchildren. My experiences in both business and family motivate me to inspire women to embrace their strength and creativity. Through my work, I aim to make a positive impact in the lives of those around me, encouraging them to pursue their dreams and stand strong in their journeys.

The Importance of Female Entrepreneurship in Today's Society

By Nytisha Davis

Female entrepreneurs play a crucial role in the economy by establishing businesses that create jobs and generate wealth. This has always been something I care about deeply, especially because I wanted to set a good example for my two daughters. When I was a young mother, I wanted to provide them with a better life and show them that there were many paths to success. I believe in the power of creating multiple sources of income, so they can see that there are different ways to support themselves and achieve their dreams. My goal is to inspire my daughters and now four granddaughters, and help them understand the opportunities available to them.

The Spark of Inspiration

From a young age, I felt a strong desire inside me, a small flame of ambition that hinted I could be an entrepreneur. I always believed I was meant to do something special and make a real difference in the world. While I could imagine success, I found it hard to figure out what that would look like. Still, I held onto the belief that my journey would lead me to something important.

Growing up, I realized that traditional paths often felt limiting. The idea of settling for a regular 9-to-5 job with a set salary seemed suffocating to me. I always wanted to push boundaries and challenge the norm. This restlessness fueled my drive and pushed me to seek opportunities that would let me explore my potential. I never wanted to accept an average life; I craved the freedom to create my own path.

I believed that "the sky's the limit." This mindset led me to try different ways to succeed, whether through creative projects, side gigs, or starting my own business. As I searched for fulfillment, I explored various interests, each helping me understand myself better. I surrounded myself with positive influences—mentors, books, and groups of like-minded people who inspired me to think bigger and dream more boldly.

At first, I thought of success mainly in terms of money. I believed that my achievements would be measured by how much I could earn. I chased opportunities that promised high financial returns, thinking that wealth would bring me happiness. However, as I moved along this path, I realized that true success goes beyond just money.

Over time, my view of success changed. I began to measure it by the quality of life I was creating for myself—mind, body, and soul. I learned that real fulfillment comes from following passions that align with my values and contribute to my sense of purpose. I started to focus on my well-being, understanding that a balanced life is key to my overall happiness and effectiveness as an entrepreneur.

This shift in how I define success has been life-changing. It has encouraged me to align my business goals with my core beliefs and passions. I began to pursue projects that not only offered financial rewards but also allowed me to express my creativity, help my community, and make a positive impact on others' lives.

As I think back on my early influences and inspirations, I see how they have shaped my entrepreneurial spirit. The spark that ignited my ambition still drives me forward, guiding me as I navigate the ups and downs of entrepreneurship. I'm committed to facing challenges, learning from setbacks, and celebrating every small victory as I work to create a life that reflects my vision of success.

Ultimately, my journey as an entrepreneur shows the power of believing in yourself and following your passions. I'm grateful for the influences that have helped shape me, and I'm excited to keep exploring the endless possibilities ahead as I carve my path in the world of entrepreneurship.

Eliminating and Overcoming Self-Doubt

There's an African proverb that says, "When there is no enemy within, the enemy outside can do you no harm." This means that when you truly believe in yourself, you take control of your own future. In that powerful moment, what others think becomes less important; they cannot decide who you will be. Only you have that power, and only you can choose the direction of your life. To achieve your dreams, you must be prepared to fight for them against those who might try to bring you down. These can include skeptics, critics, and even people close to you who, despite their good intentions, might unintentionally hold you back.

The journey to believing in yourself can be tough. There can be a long wait between thinking about your goals and actually taking action. This is often when doubt sneaks in, and hesitation can take hold. Have you ever shared a "great idea" with someone, only to feel regret afterward? It can be discouraging when their response is filled with doubt or concerns about what can't be done. Instead of getting support, you might find yourself struggling with self-doubt, feeling like your vision isn't understood or valued.

This experience taught me the importance of keeping my ideas private. My vision is unique to me, and while I sometimes want to share it, I've realized I need to protect it from outside opinions. The world can be noisy, filled with voices that echo feelings of inadequacy and judgment. It's easy to get caught up in thoughts like, "I'm not good enough" or "I don't deserve success." These negative thoughts can create a powerful sense of doubt that stops us from moving forward.

The biggest challenge we face is often fighting against our own doubts. It's not just about dealing with what others say; it's also about overcoming the negative thoughts in our own minds. To get past this, we need to learn how to control our thoughts. This means actively replacing negative ideas with positive affirmations. It's important to develop a mindset that values self-worth and resilience.

Setting goals is important, but having meaningful goals is even more powerful. These are goals that connect with your values and passions, leading you toward fulfillment. Work on yourself every day to quiet the noise of self-doubt. Engage in activities that support your mental and emotional well-being—whether it's meditation, journaling, or being around positive people.

Every morning, I start my day by watching motivational videos and listening to podcasts. This routine has become a key part of my life, giving me inspiration that fuels my entrepreneurial journey. In the fast-paced world of business, where challenges are common, surrounding myself with uplifting messages is essential for staying motivated and focused. It's important to cut out negativity and replace it with activities that empower you.

Empowerment means setting yourself up for success. It's about creating an environment where your dreams can grow. Invest time in yourself, seek knowledge, and embrace experiences that align with your vision. Understand that the journey may not always be easy, but every step you take shows your commitment to believing in yourself and growing as a person.

Ultimately, the path to achieving your dreams requires courage. You need to rise above doubts, both from others and from yourself, and champion your vision with determination. When you believe in yourself, you light the way forward, allowing you to create a life that is truly yours. Remember, you hold the pen to your own story. Write it confidently, and let your journey inspire those around you.

Learning the Ropes: My Journey to Understanding My Business Brand

It's important to really know your business brand. I made an effort to learn as much as I could by attending networking events, watching YouTube videos, and reading books suggested by successful entrepreneurs. I also took the time to understand the language used in the industry and did the necessary work to get familiar with it.

I joined social media groups related to my business to see how others tackle similar challenges I faced. During car rides to appointments, I listened to helpful podcasts. To learn more, I even applied for a job at a competing company just to see how their business worked. All these steps helped me gain valuable insights into my own business.

Navigating Challenges and Setbacks

As I embarked on my journey to become an entrepreneur, I had a clear vision of how I wanted to live my life. My ultimate goal was to achieve complete independence—financially, creatively, and personally. I envisioned a future where I could build a business that not only fulfilled my ambitions but also allowed me to live authentically on my own terms. With this vision in mind, I set a timeline for myself, believing that my dreams were within reach.

At first, everything seemed to be falling into place. I took the necessary steps to establish my business, setting up my LLC, obtaining my EIN, and launching a website that showcased my offerings. I was filled with excitement and optimism, ready to embrace the challenges and rewards that came with entrepreneurship. However, as is often the case in the entrepreneurial world, life threw me a curveball just a few months in.

I experienced a significant financial setback that led me to contemplate closing my business. The weight of my responsibilities outside of my entrepreneurial pursuits felt overwhelming, and I found myself questioning whether I could continue. The pressure of financial obligations weighed heavily on my shoulders, and the thought of putting my dreams on the back burner loomed large. In that moment of doubt, I felt as if my aspirations were slipping away.

Yet, during this challenging period, my spouse became my unwavering source of encouragement. He believed in my vision and urged me not to give up on my dreams. His support reminded me that every setback is a part of the journey, and sometimes, the road to success is paved with obstacles that test our resolve. With his encouragement, I decided to keep moving forward, even when the path seemed uncertain.

To help alleviate the financial strain, I took on a second job. This decision was not easy, as it meant dedicating additional hours to work outside of my business. However, it was a necessary step to offset the costs of supplies and keep my entrepreneurial dream alive. Each week, I meticulously planned my schedule, balancing my responsibilities while ensuring that I dedicated time to my business. It was a juggling act that required discipline, focus, minimal sleep, and sacrifice.

There were moments when discouragement crept in, especially during times when I felt like I was not making progress. I often found myself questioning whether I would ever see the light at the end of the tunnel. However, it was my faith and spiritual relationship with God that provided me with the strength to persevere. In those moments of uncertainty, I leaned on my faith, finding solace in the belief that my hard work and dedication would eventually yield results.

Additionally, I recognized the importance of surrounding myself with like-minded individuals who shared my passion and motivation. I connected with other entrepreneurs who were navigating their own journeys, and together, we uplifted one another. This community became a vital part of my support system, providing encouragement, sharing resources, and exchanging ideas. Being in the company of others who understood the challenges of entrepreneurship kept my spirits high and reinforced my belief in my own potential.

Through this journey, I learned that entrepreneurship is not just about having a great idea; it's about resilience, adaptability, and faith in oneself. Each challenge I faced became a lesson in perseverance, and every small victory fueled my determination to keep going. My path to independence is still unfolding, but I am more committed than ever to pursuing my dreams and building a life that reflects my true self. With faith, support, and hard work, I know that I can overcome any obstacle that stands in my way.

The Purpose of Building a Brand: Finding Your Story and Your Why

When I decided to start my own business, I quickly realized how important it was to understand the purpose behind my brand. I had to ask myself some key questions: *What is my story? Why am I starting this business?* These questions were crucial because they would shape the foundation of my brand and guide my choices moving forward.

I needed to think about why I wanted to focus on this specific area. It wasn't just because I had worked in the industry for a long time; it was much deeper than that. After gaining experience in different roles, I discovered a strong desire to provide a service that genuinely made life easier for people, based on their lifestyles and individual needs. This insight became a key reason for my entrepreneurial journey.

You may have heard the saying, "Your WHY should be what drives you." This idea really struck a chord with me. Your WHY should capture the essence of your motivation—something you can explain easily, like in a "two-minute elevator pitch." We've all seen movies where an aspiring entrepreneur gets a quick chance to pitch their idea in an elevator. They have only a few moments to explain what they offer and why it's important before the doors open.

Someone once told me that if I met a potential client or investor in an elevator, I should be ready to share my WHY and the value I can provide in just two minutes. At first, I found it challenging to express those thoughts clearly. I knew I wanted to start a business and that I had a passion for helping people, but I hadn't fully figured out my story yet.

My initial WHY came from a personal experience that greatly influenced my perspective. My father was diagnosed with colon cancer, and during his treatment, he often needed routine blood work. This required him to spend long hours waiting at a Patient Service Center (PSC). I offered to come to his home to do the bloodwork, hoping to make things easier for him, but he always refused. For him, those visits to the PSC were a chance to get some fresh air and a break from his treatment routine.

Having worked as a phlebotomist and mobile phlebotomist for many years, I found it more rewarding to help patients who were homebound. There was something fulfilling about assisting those who struggled to care for themselves. My experiences in the industry helped me develop important skills, but my previous work as a caregiver taught me valuable lessons in patience and compassion.

Think about the families who trust you with the care of their loved ones. What kind of service would you want to provide them? This question guided my approach to building my brand. I realized that my passion for helping others, combined with my experience, could lead to a business that not only offers a service but also shows empathy and understanding.

As a result, my brand was created from a mix of personal experience and professional dedication. It reflects my commitment to making a positive impact in the lives of those I serve. By sharing my story and explaining my WHY, I've been able to build a brand that aligns with my values and mission—one that is focused on compassion, support, and the desire to make life a little easier for others. As I continue on this entrepreneurial journey, I remain dedicated to refining my story, ensuring it stays at the heart of everything I do.

Breaking Down Barriers While Making a Social Impact

As a woman of color, I have faced many challenges throughout my life that have shaped who I am today. I was born in the 1970s, a time when women and people of color faced significant difficulties. Growing up in a world filled with inequalities, I saw firsthand the struggles many of us dealt with because of our race and gender.

During my childhood, opportunities were often limited, and there were strict expectations from society. Women, especially women of color, were often undervalued, and their contributions were overlooked. The barriers we faced were not just personal; they were built into society itself. From education to job opportunities, there were obstacles everywhere that made it hard for us to follow our dreams.

While some progress has been made since the 1970s and certain barriers are less visible now, many challenges still exist today. The fight for equality continues, and the struggles faced by women of color have changed but have not disappeared. For example, while outright discrimination may happen less often than in the past, there are still subtle biases and systemic barriers that affect our chances and experiences.

I have always disliked limitations and restrictions in my life, which has led me to develop a habit of breaking barriers. If someone tells me that I can't do something, it only motivates me to find a way to prove them wrong. I thrive on challenges and view them as opportunities to show what I'm capable of.

When I'm in a group, I often find myself wanting to go against the crowd. If everyone is heading in one direction, I tend to choose a different path. This instinct comes from my desire for independence and my belief in following my own instincts rather than simply going along with what others want. I believe that true growth comes from stepping outside of one's comfort zone and exploring new possibilities, even if it means standing apart from the group.

This mindset has shaped my journey and pushed me to take risks that have ultimately led to personal growth and fulfillment. I embrace challenges and see them as chances to prove my strengths and capabilities.

Today, women of color continue to face challenges in the workplace, including lower pay, fewer opportunities for leadership positions, and limited chances to network and advance in their careers. While these issues may not be as overt as the discrimination of the past, they still create significant obstacles for us.

It's Okay to Take a Break

During my journey to becoming an entrepreneur, I faced many challenges that became overwhelming. As I entered the second year of my business, the pressure from deadlines, marketing tasks, and my full-time job started to take a toll on me. There were times when I felt I was making progress towards my goals, only to experience setbacks that made me question my efforts. I often thought, *What's the point?* But I pushed through because I knew I had come too far to give up.

I would come home late from my second job and head straight to my office, working on my business well into the early hours of the morning. With only a few hours of sleep before my next day at the 9-to-5, I was running on caffeine and determination. While my business began to grow, my body was sending me signals that I needed to pay attention.

Being a bit of a workaholic, I was always eager to start new projects and tasks. However, I learned early on that it's important to listen to your body. Understanding how your body feels when it's healthy versus when it's run down is crucial. I realized that taking a break is not a sign of weakness but a necessary part of maintaining well-being.

Initially, the thought of taking time off stressed me out because it felt like I was risking potential earnings. Eventually, I made the tough decision to reduce my hours at my job to dedicate more time to my business. This change also meant I would commit to a self-care day every week, a day where I focus solely on myself. On that day, I step away from work duties to go to the gym, treat myself to a pedicure, enjoy a massage, or relax with a good book.

I've discovered that when I seek clarity or answers, sitting in silence often helps me find the solutions I need. Taking time for myself has not only improved my well-being but has also allowed me to approach my business with a clearer mind.

In Conclusion

Embrace your weaknesses and turn them into your strengths. Everyone has areas where they struggle, but these challenges can help us grow and learn. Instead of feeling defeated by your shortcomings, see them as opportunities to develop new skills and become a stronger person.

Think of your journey as a path to success. Each step you take, whether easy or difficult, is part of your unique story. Celebrate the progress you make along the way, even if it feels small. Every experience, good or bad, contributes to who you are and leads you to your victories.

Make your journey a source of inspiration for yourself. You have the power to create a story that reflects your resilience and determination.

Share your experiences with others, showing how you overcame obstacles and transformed challenges into triumphs. Your journey can motivate not just you but also others who may be facing similar struggles.

Recognize that your weaknesses don't define you; they're just part of your story. By acknowledging and overcoming them, you can write a victory story that showcases your strength and perseverance.

It can be discouraging and intimidating to push past those who try to deny you a seat at the table. However, it's important to remember that you deserve a place at that table. If the existing table does not welcome you, then create your own table where you have the power to decide who sits at it. By doing this, you take control of your opportunities and ensure that your voice is heard. Empower yourself and others by building an inclusive space where everyone can thrive.

My name is Nytisha Davis, and I am the owner and founder of Hobo Bay-Be LLC, the designer of my new shoe line, Na'tash Shoes, and the founder and CEO of Phillips Mobile Labs LLC. At Phillips Mobile Labs, we are passionate about developing new and innovative solutions, and we are excited about expanding our brand. As an extension of our brand, we will also bring focus on promoting women's health, and we want to introduce products and services that support and empower women in their everyday lives.

Annette Mashi

Founder of Write Wizards

https://linkedin.com/in/annettemashi
https://www.facebook.com/annette.mashi
https://www.instagram.com/annettemashi/
https://www.writewizards.com/

Annette Mashi, founder of Write Wizards, creates magic with words. She's an enchanting copywriter and content strategist for creative female business coaches, consultants, and designers. She highlights their superpowers and tells their stories, promoting their unique charms. She increases their visibility by cutting through the noise and positioning them as experts and thought leaders. Escaping from an international corporate high-tech company, Annette has been casting her spells for female entrepreneurs looking to stand out and make a more significant impact. Annette writes website copy, nurturing emails, and sales sequences to attract and convert their dream clients. With her mystical process, she captures your authentic voice so the writing resonates with your readers as if it were conjured by your own hands.

Resilient Magic: From Corporate America to War-Time Entrepreneurship

By Annette Mashi

I can't imagine living anywhere else. Even with the war raging and the unpredictable barrage of rocket attacks, Israel is my home. There's a constant threat of terrorist attacks, yet it's the country I feel safest. Here, people support each other in amazing displays of unity. And we defend each other, not afraid to sacrifice ourselves.

I didn't always feel this way. I was born and raised in the suburbs of Philadelphia, the oldest of 5 kids—an overachiever, people-pleaser, good girl, rule follower. My path seemed planned. Finish high school with honors, attend Drexel for computer science, get a decent, well-paying job, and find a nice Jewish husband.

Computer coding wasn't for me, so I tapped into my creative side and studied architecture. I was full of self-doubt and wondered who would hire me to design their dream home. I put architecture on the "back burner" and focused on computer support.

I was also looking for love, naive enough to assume a nice Jewish boy would make my dreams come true. I was introduced to an Israeli that my friends recommended.

"What's wrong with him?" I asked. But Tzion met 90% of my "husband" criteria; we loved each other and, within 6 months, were married.

We discussed moving to Israel, the Jewish homeland, where his family was.

Being Jewish is important to me. I wanted my children to have an easier time finding spouses. The holidays would be "my" holidays, without competition between Hanukkah and Christmas. I thought I would feel more at home in Israel.

I jumped in without considering the situation and took a huge risk.

I hadn't thought about my feelings living so far from home. I didn't know the language. Instead of planning, I jumped into the unknown. I still can't believe I was brave enough.

Moving to Israel

We took our one-year-old daughter and started our lives in Israel. I left everything I knew: my family, friends, and home. I felt alone and isolated. I didn't have a job or speak the language. And we moved in with my in-laws.

28 years ago, there was no internet, Zoom, or FaceTime. Everything was different. I couldn't communicate and struggled to fit in. I felt invisible and unheard, without a voice.

When Intel hired me, I thought I had found my place. I was challenged to solve problems and explain solutions by phone in a foreign language. The software was in English, but all the team meetings were in Hebrew. I skipped lunches to avoid feeling isolated by not understanding the conversations.

Forming friendships with the language barrier was hard, and I felt lonely.

I struggled with infertility, crying into my pillow with no one to talk to. I felt like a failure. I couldn't control the situation, as I tried again and again to get pregnant. I finally realized that I was lucky to have two beautiful daughters. I summoned my resilience and embraced the family I had created, overcoming the thought that my worth wasn't measured by my ability to have more children.

Working at Intel

Due to the pain of infertility, I focused less on my family and more on my career, working hard in a male-dominated, high-tech environment. There were projects, deadlines, and late-night meetings.

Intel was a golden cage. Everything was at the facility—dry cleaning, nail salon, and fitness center, so employees would never have to leave. The management emphasized that it was a "Great Place to Work."

They gave us little surprises to keep us motivated. The people I worked with were like family. We brought our children to holiday parties and special events at zoos, amusement parks, and water playgrounds. Mostly, I was happy and unaware that life could be different.

I was a dedicated employee. I assumed I was appreciated and would be compensated accordingly.

But that wasn't the case. On a yearly review, though I was up for a promotion, I was passed over. Instead, my manager promoted a single guy. The explanation was that I was married with two kids and less likely to leave. Again, I felt unseen, unheard, invisible.

I was devastated but pushed it aside and continued taking on more responsibilities. I oversaw the capital budget of $36M to buy computers for all employees globally.

When the economy changed, Intel started a cycle of layoffs. What was once "job security" with a good company had turned into fear and anxiety. It was a matter of time before it was my turn.

I could choose to stay or go. My manager encouraged me to leave, and I felt rejected, so I left. Intel took 17 years of my life. All my friends were there. Working at Intel was my identity, and it determined my wealth and value. I felt lost, unsure of what to do next. My confidence was shaken, and I wondered how I could rebuild myself.

Finding My Next Steps

Once unemployed, I finally took the opportunity to think about my life and my abilities. What skills did I have from the past 50 years? What did I enjoy, and what made me happy?

I tried teaching English to kids in the local junior high. That lasted 6 days and was awful. I cried daily. Teaching adults English was also challenging. They quickly lost interest or became frustrated, and I struggled to find steady clients. Self-doubt plagued me as I explored my path forward.

I turned to writing since I had always been a word wizard.

I remember helping my 16-year-old sister with her résumé. I titled her "beverage coordinator." She worked at McDonald's, asking customers if they wanted Coke, Sprite, or orange soda.

At Intel, I helped people with yearly reviews. I used words like analyzed, optimized, and implemented to make employees sound important. I also created presentations, showing results and influencing decision-making.

I became a freelancer for a company that teaches architects and interior designers marketing skills. I created blogs, newsletters, and website copy with each designer's style, words, and tone so the content messages would attract their dream clients. I wrote to show the architect's expertise and thought leadership.

After years of feeling unseen and unheard, I prevented others from feeling that way. I wrote words that give my clients a voice, make them visible, and highlight their superpowers.

Life as a Female Entrepreneur

I didn't plan to start a business. However, I enjoyed my freedom, choosing how to spend my day. The flexibility was exhilarating. But I had no experience as a business owner. I didn't know how to find clients or what to offer. I knew very little about marketing, sales, and pricing my services.

Working alone was lonely, with no one to talk to, and I spent hours in front of the computer.

The pandemic made me feel more isolated, so I joined an online networking group. I discovered like-minded individuals who were running their businesses. We could share ideas and learn from each other.

I also hired a business coach and connected with other female entrepreneurs. We talked about how to increase visibility. I began tracking my time, developing a marketing strategy, and understanding my business finances.

At Intel, I only had to do my job. As a female entrepreneur, I became the marketing, sales, and finance departments.

There was awareness of everything I didn't know, and I tried to close the gaps. I listened to podcasts, took training courses, and joined a writing society to improve my copy and content skills.

Online networking replaced the emptiness I felt. I connected with other women to learn about them and their businesses. I built relationships and strategic partners (women who worked with the same clients as me).

I removed the "everything is wonderful" mask and shared my self-doubts and fears. I welcomed the insight of others to overcome my struggles. I gratefully accepted words of wisdom and passed on my expertise to others. I realized that there is no competition. Everyone has their way of running their business with their own secret sauce.

Through these communities, I finally felt the power to be visible, courageous, and successful.

We are so much stronger when we help each other rise. We energize and inspire to become unstoppable. Each issue we face is not a failure but an opportunity to learn and grow. Having supportive communities helped me personally and professionally thrive.

Living in a War Zone

On October 7, 2023, everything changed.

I remember banging on my daughter's door to wake her up and quickly opening the front door for our little black dog, Max. We entered the bomb shelter. I had no idea what was coming and the amount of devastation ahead. I watched the tragedy unfold in disbelief.

Even today, 15 months later, I still feel the raw pain and anguish, writing to you and blinking back the tears that are streaming down my face.

The loss of innocent lives, the bravery of the soldiers, the heart-wrenching stories of hostages—is worse than a nightmare. My heart aches for the 1200 people who died that dreadful day, including my friend Ricarda's daughter, Shani, a vibrant soul who loved to dance.

Running my business was far from my mind. Paralysis set in. I felt unbelievably depressed as if my life had been sucked out of my body. I couldn't eat, couldn't sleep, and could barely move.

Marketing was impossible. I couldn't post on social media. I had no voice. I felt like I could scream for days at the top of my lungs, but no sound would come out. Even as a writer, I had no words. What could I possibly write about that is as important as life and death?

The feeling of emptiness was so overwhelming. It was as if I was reliving the pain of the death of my parents multiplied by 100 times.

Life in Israel went on as we fought for survival. I watched my daughter's fiancé, Roy, put on his army clothes and go off to serve. He attached metal tags to his boots so that if anything happened to him, his body could be identified. I tried to put on a brave face as I hugged him and told him to stay safe. He packed supplies, not knowing when he would return, and my husband drove him 35 minutes to the base while rockets were exploding overhead.

I felt helpless, constantly listening to the television for news, tracking the missiles, and praying that I wouldn't have to run for cover. (I have 45 seconds to get to a protected area.)

This became my new reality, the turbulence of living in a war zone.

Controlling What I Could

I started each client meeting with these exact words. *"In the event of an alarm in my area, I'll have to stop our call and go into my bomb shelter for at least 10 minutes. Then I'll call you back."*

As I met with my clients, I focused on our conversations. I gathered their information to write emails, articles, and social media posts to market their businesses. And then, I would write, putting all my emotions aside and pouring my heart into their content.

The sound of artillery shells and the roar of the air force jets overhead was constant. Max never left my side (terrified of the booming). I sat at my desk, creating magic with words and content my clients needed to market themselves.

I temporarily closed my mind to the names and faces of the soldiers who are dying daily. I suppressed the images of the female hostages and blocked off thoughts of what they might be suffering. I limited the amount of news and social media to prevent myself from being sucked into the abyss.

I watched the families of the hostages traveling around the globe, pleading for the release of their daughters, sons, fathers, brothers, and sisters. I allowed myself to feel helpless, to grieve, and I let the tears fall from my eyes.

Then, I shook it off as best I could—knowing that surviving and thriving is the best revenge.

The backlash from clients abroad who have different views on what is happening in Israel caused a loss of business. There was no choice but to rise above negative feelings and hatred to keep my business moving forward.

Focusing on Joy and Happiness

Despite the hardships and constant threat of rockets, we can't let those who want to destroy us win. We continue our lives through the uncertainty, taking opportunities to celebrate and rejoice.

During the war, both my daughters got married. Flights were canceled, and we had to scramble to find alternative ways for my sisters from the US to attend the weddings. The fear that my son-in-law would be called to reserve duty loomed overhead.

As the brides prepared for their wedding days, the planes overhead and artillery noise were a stark reminder of the chaos beyond our celebration.

However, I consciously decided to enjoy the wedding days, savoring the precious moments.

I closed my eyes to take snapshots reflecting the joy in my daughters' smiling faces as they descended the stairs in their wedding dresses. I appreciated the laughter as we curled our hair, applied our makeup, and fastened our elegant necklaces and sparkling earrings.

I cried tears of happiness as Orlee and Saar walked down the aisle to stand under the wedding canopy. And smiled from ear to ear as Tzion and I walked Leah down the aisle to her awaiting groom, Roy.

There's an inherent whirlwind of emotions on any wedding day, so I focused on finding solace and joy while proving that love and happiness can flourish even in the darkest times.

Being Resilient Brings Happiness

As I look back, the word that comes to mind is resilience. You can learn to pick up the pieces and live in a new reality. Sometimes, your heart aches with so much pain and tears. That's when you dig deep within yourself and focus on being joyous, even temporarily.

I have found my passion: creating magic with words. I give a voice to those who feel silent, unseen, and unheard. I aim to highlight other women when they are too full of self-doubt to promote their superpowers.

Through my journey, I've learned that resilience isn't just about personal strength—it's about building connections that sustain us through life's uncertainties.

Concentrate on what you can control. Lean on the strength of your communities so you never feel alone. Connect with people you love and who love you for support on your journey.

No one knows what the future will hold. Life is full of uncertainty. When we make plans, we only fool ourselves into a false sense of security. Seek happiness, even if the world around you appears to be crumbling.

I want to thank everyone who has expressed concern for my safety, given me encouraging support during these turbulent times, and lifted my spirits when I needed it most.

Lilly Kruzsely

Founder of Harmonix LLC

https://www.linkedin.com/company/harmonix-llc
https://www.facebook.com/profile.php?id=61554300496755#
https://open.spotify.com/artist/4jiEIBWJfz7bOp6Chhz6TG

Lilly Kruzsely is the founder of Harmonix LLC, an innovative A.I. think tank dedicated to empowering artists in the rapidly evolving landscape of artificial intelligence. With a mission to demystify the "scary" world of A.I., Lilly and Harmonix LLC help artists integrate cutting-edge A.I. solutions into their creative processes, offering tools and strategies they might not have previously considered. As a young entrepreneur, Lilly is passionate about globally influencing youth to reach their fullest potential, fostering a new generation of creators who harness the power of technology for artistic growth and expression.

Walk a Mile

By Lilly Kruzsely

By all means, the story you are about to read must be disclaimed as fiction, subject to conflict of interest clauses. Yet, I invite you to step into my world, to walk a mile in my shoes, and follow the path that led me to founding my business, Harmonix LLC—a path I vowed never to retrace, shaped by experiences I refuse to endure again.

For four years after graduating from the University of Ottawa, I had the honor of serving Canadians as an executive assistant to a senator at the Senate of Canada. It was, without question, the best job I had ever held—at least, initially. I worked on legislation that had the power to change lives, particularly for Canadians with disabilities—Canadians like me. Every day, bright-eyed and determined, I ascended the grand steps of Parliament Hill, carrying the weight of my own battles yet driven by the hope of a better future. Not just for my country, but for the 350,000 Canadians who shared my reality.

Type 1. Insulin-dependent. Diabetic.

This is where my journey truly begins.

There are no words to fully capture how dehumanizing my experience at the Senate of Canada became—and, as I understand it, still is to this day. I told myself I would never go back unless I saw a parliamentarian's seat filled by someone just like me.

Once, I believed I could be Canada's first insulin-dependent type 1 diabetic parliamentarian. Now, I'm not so sure that anyone like me can be. This illness turns life into a relentless battle, and my time within those walls forced me to confront a brutal question: Does the intersection of marginalization and systemic oversight make it impossible for people like me to serve in Canada's highest offices?

Canada is the country where insulin was discovered, yet nowhere in its history can I find a record of a type 1 diabetic ever holding a seat in Parliament. I've combed through debates, Hansards, government records, news releases, called offices, written letters, and pursued personal conversations—all leading to the same unsettling silence, the same glaring absence.

Just sit with that for a moment.

What drove me to seek this answer with such intensity? The refusal, over the course of my entire four-year tenure, to install a single safe sharps disposal bin anywhere within the Senate precinct. A basic, essential biohazardous waste container.

This refusal persisted even after the passage of a national diabetes strategy. It persisted even after the Accessible Canada Act became law. And still, I fought for this basic accommodation. And I failed. Miserably.

The irony was a cruel twist of the knife. I worked in an office that was well known for championing the rights of persons with disabilities, contributing to legislation intended to dismantle barriers and pave the way for a more inclusive Canada. Yet—in an office known for championing the rights of persons with disabilities—I was met with a stark, undeniable truth: even in a space theoretically designed to advocate for people like me, my specific, essential needs were invisible, inconsequential. It felt as though my disability, the very essence of my daily struggle, was a footnote, a minor inconvenience easily dismissed. How could it possibly matter, I reasoned with growing despair, when no parliamentarian had ever walked this path, had ever lived this reality?

The lack of a simple sharps disposal bin became a daily, tangible symbol of this profound indifference. It wasn't just an inconvenience; it was a constant hazard. Every day, I carried my used needles, my biohazardous waste, home in my purse—a gnawing reminder of my "otherness." The fear of accidental needle pricks became a familiar, unwelcome companion. Reaching for my apartment keys, I'd often feel the sharp, used tip of a needle brush against my fingers, a small but potent reminder of the precariousness forced upon me. It was a daily gamble, a silent, internal scream against the systemic disregard.

The sharps disposal bin was not the only absence. There were other, less tangible, but equally significant, instances of inaccessibility. The subtle, unspoken assumptions that my needs were somehow "extra," that my daily management of a chronic illness was an imposition. The constant, quiet pressure to conform to a standard of "normal" that simply didn't exist for me. It was in the raised eyebrows when I had to step away for a moment to manage my blood sugar, the hushed whispers when I discreetly injected insulin before a meal. It was in the implicit message, carried in the very air of the Senate, that my body, my reality, was a problem to be minimized, ignored, or, at best, tolerated.

And then there was the silence. My silence.

Until today, I never told anyone. Not a coworker, not a superior, not a single soul within those walls. To reveal the daily indignities, the constant struggle, the physical risks I was forced to take, felt like admitting defeat. It felt like confirming the unspoken narrative that my presence was a burden, that my needs were unreasonable. I carried the weight of it alone, a secret shame festering within the very institution I had so desperately wanted to serve. The fear of being seen as "difficult," as "demanding," as "too much," was a heavy, suffocating blanket.

The question lingered, a constant, gnawing ache: What hope was there for the rest of Canada? If the Senate, the supposed pinnacle of our democracy, couldn't make space for a type 1 diabetic to serve Canadians in an inclusive way, what chance did anyone else navigating similar challenges have?

This silent battle, this constant navigation of a system designed, however unintentionally, to exclude me, became the crucible in which my disillusionment was forged. The dream of serving as a parliamentarian, once so bright and unwavering, began to dim under the weight of systemic indifference. The sheer exhaustion of fighting a battle that seemed unwinnable, a battle I couldn't even speak aloud, began to take its toll.

"Dehumanizing." The word, though accurate, still feels insufficient to capture the depth of the emotional wound. It wasn't just about the lack of a sharps disposal bin or the subtle, dismissive glances. It was about the insidious erosion of my sense of self, the relentless whisper that I was somehow less than, that my contributions were inherently diminished by my body's needs. It was a constant, gnawing feeling of being erased, of being rendered invisible within the very institution I had pledged my loyalty and skills to.

The experience left me with a profound sense of trauma, a lingering PTSD that manifested in vivid, recurring nightmares. In the darkness of sleep, I relived the indignities, the silent battles, the crushing weight of indifference. I often woke with a renewed sense of despair, grappling with the deep-seated fear that I had nothing of value left to offer Canada, or my fellow Canadians. The sense of isolation was profound. It felt as though I was adrift, abandoned, left to navigate a world that seemed determined to pretend people like me didn't exist in positions of influence.

There were moments, dark and desperate, when I felt a chilling, visceral sense of abandonment. A feeling that perhaps type 1 diabetics were simply meant to be discarded, that our lives were perceived as a burden, an inconvenience best kept out of sight. The invention of insulin, discovered here in Canada, once a symbol of hope and life, twisted into a cruel mockery in my mind. It no longer felt like just a lifeline; it sometimes felt like a tool of false hope, a way to prolong suffering by shifting the burden of care from the sterile confines of a hospital to the unforgiving reality of a society unwilling to fully accommodate us. It felt, in those dark moments, like insulin was invented not just for us, but to make doctors feel better about the children they saved, only to send them out into a world that would rather they didn't exist, leaving us someone else's problem.

The relentless battle with diabetes, already a daily struggle, was amplified exponentially by the toxic stress of the Senate environment. I didn't fully comprehend the extent of the physical damage until the COVID-19 pandemic forced us to work from home. The change was stark, almost unbelievable. My basal insulin requirements—the background insulin my body needs constantly—plummeted by 40%. Forty percent! Logic dictated that with less physical activity, more takeout meals supporting local businesses, and the general stress of a global pandemic, my insulin needs should have increased, or at least stayed the same. But the opposite was true. The sheer, suffocating stress of the Senate workplace, the constant, invisible pressure of navigating that inaccessible environment, had been wreaking havoc on my body. It had been forcing me to pump myself full of significantly more insulin just to survive the workday. The dramatic drop was stark, undeniable proof of the environment's toxicity.

This wasn't just about inconvenience or hurt feelings. It was about survival. It was about the very real, measurable, physical impact of systemic indifference and exclusion. It was the devastating realization that the institution I had so desperately wanted to serve, the place I had poured my heart and energy into, was, in fact, slowly killing me.

The disillusionment wasn't just a feeling anymore; it was a cold, hard certainty, solidified by the undeniable physical evidence of my body's reaction when removed from that toxic environment. The 40% drop in my insulin needs working from home wasn't just data; it was proof that the Senate stress, the constant navigation of an inaccessible system, was literally harming me. This physical reality, combined with the emotional scars of feeling dehumanized, the PTSD, the recurring nightmares, and the profound isolation, painted a bleak picture. Added to that was the stark realization of the systemic barriers—the historical lack of representation, the troubling implications of MAiD criteria, the disparities in insulin access based on province or delivery method. It wasn't just about a sharps bin anymore; it was about recognizing that the entire structure, the very system I aspired to join, felt fundamentally incompatible with my survival, let alone my ability to thrive and serve effectively. The dream of becoming Canada's first type 1 diabetic parliamentarian wasn't just dimmed; it felt completely extinguished, revealed as an impossibility within the existing, exclusionary framework.

The intersectional marginalization felt too vast—how could I aspire to that seat when basic access wasn't guaranteed, when even the types of insulin available differ based on factors unrelated to medical need, favoring pump users with biologic insulin while injection users living in the province of Ontario like me are relegated to biosimilars lacking long-term study data? The system felt rigged, not just indifferent.

So, what do you do when the path you envisioned crumbles beneath your feet? When the institution you believed in reveals itself to be harmful?

You listen to Lady Gaga's "Marry the Night." You pick yourself up. And you pivot.

I did it all over again, but this time, on my own terms. I looked around and asked myself: what path offers the best chance of creating change, of potentially reaching that parliamentary seat within my lifetime? A lifetime already statistically predicted to be 12–18 years shorter than average simply because of this condition? It certainly wasn't continuing down a path that was actively harming my health and spirit.

I noticed a pattern among many newly appointed senators: a foundation in business, in building something from the ground up. So, I decided I too would start laying foundations. My own foundations.

The nightmare of the Senate became the unlikely catalyst for Harmonix LLC. On paper, Harmonix LLC is an artificial intelligence (AI) think tank. But that description barely scratches the surface. It's a dynamic space for experimenting with the vast, rapidly expanding capabilities of AI. We delve into everything from generating novel creative content—yes, written works and music, but also potentially visual art, code, interactive narratives, entirely new forms of expression—to analyzing complex datasets, identifying hidden patterns, building predictive models, and exploring AI's potential to solve challenging problems. It's about pushing the boundaries, testing AI capabilities from the practical to the profound, and measuring their resonance with the public. The potential applications feel limitless, stretching across industries and aspects of human experience. As technology evolves, marching towards quantum computing, so too will Harmonix.

But Harmonix is more than just AI. It's infused with the lessons learned in the crucible of the Senate and inspired by the lifelines that got me through difficult times, including my own struggles during university—a time when the University of Ottawa, my alma mater, stopped tracking student suicide rates in 2019. Music was my sanctuary then, a vital tool for mental health. That's why Harmonix LLC also has a record label component, representing seven musical artists and championing music as a force for well-being. It's about finding harmony, both literally and figuratively.

Founding Harmonix LLC wasn't abandoning the dream of representation; it was reframing it. It was choosing to build something rather than simply fight against something. It's about creating value, exploring new frontiers, and perhaps, building the platform, the resources, and the resilience needed to one day challenge those inaccessible structures from a different position of strength.

The path is different now. It's uncertain, demanding, and entirely my own. But it's a path I walk with open eyes, carrying the lessons of the past not as insurmountable burdens, but as fuel.

The goal remains: a Canada where someone like me doesn't have to fight for a sharps bin, where their presence isn't seen as an anomaly, where they can serve at the highest levels without sacrificing their health or dignity. Harmonix LLC is the first step on this new road, a testament to the belief that even when established doors are closed, you can build your own. And perhaps, one day, that new road will lead back to Parliament Hill—not as an employee fighting for scraps of accommodation, but as an equal, ready to serve.

Stéphane-Laure Caubet, PhD

Founder and CEO of 8S2BUSINESS PTE LTD

https://www.linkedin.com/in/stephane-laure-caubet/
https://www.facebook.com/stephanelaure.caubet/
https://www.instagram.com/du.bilan.au.plan
https://8s2business.com/
https://www.8s2businessonline.com/

Dr. Stéphane-Laure CAUBET, an expert in international and European business law, has over a decade of experience in management, recruitment, and legal advisory roles within renowned institutions like the French Ministry and a UN Agency.

In 2015, she founded 8S2Business, a consulting firm specializing in organization and strategy, guiding entrepreneurs globally through all stages of development. She has successfully consulted for diverse industries, including design, architecture, retail, sports, and technology, serving international organizations, embassies, corporations, startups, and SMEs.

As the author of A Business Planner for the Business Starter, she is a professor, mentor, and advocate for innovation and entrepreneurship.

Her impact extends to board membership in international non-profits, highlighting her commitment to peace and responsible practices.

From Discomfort to Transformation

By Stéphane-Laure Caubet, PhD

Life is filled with contradictions, yet upon closer look, we discover that these challenges serve as stepping stones that help us see ourselves in new ways.

How Our Environment Shapes Our Beliefs

I never imagined becoming an entrepreneur—it wasn't even on my radar. My mother emphasised the importance of having a job and being financially independent, especially as a woman. She made it clear that we should never depend on a spouse or anyone else.

This emphasis on steady employment, combined with the French mindset toward social protection, shaped my perspective. Growing up in France, entrepreneurship was rarely presented as a viable career path.

Despite following a legal career path, where being a lawyer could theoretically offer freedom, I likely would have chosen the security of being hired in a salaried lawyer position.

Uncertainty is often the scariest thing: how to deal with the fact of not knowing, but life itself is wrapped in uncertainty.

We're also afraid of freedom because we know it comes at a price— one we're not always willing to pay.

If there's one thing I've learned through years of entrepreneurial experience (and life itself), it's that while we think we know ourselves, it's actually our journey that reveals who we are. Through adversity, ups and downs, and encounters both good and bad, we're constantly evolving, though fear of change can make some resist this natural transformation.

What if Our Destiny Isn't What We Imagine It Should Be?

As a little girl, I suffered from motion sickness. Whether by air, land, or sea, if I spent more than 15 minutes in any moving vehicle, I would inevitably become ill until reaching my destination.

Yet ironically, I love travelling. I've explored extensively, driven both by my dual cultural heritage and my passion for adventure and discovering new places.

Today, I live abroad and constantly use various modes of transport—from tuk-tuks in Phnom Penh to buses in Binh Duong and planes when visiting family.

Similarly striking was my extreme shyness as a child. Who would have predicted that I would not only lecture at university but also teach public speaking?

As I've matured, I've learned that life rarely follows our exact plans. While things occasionally unfold as expected, more often it's the unexpected challenges that emerge along the way, and it's these that will build and solidify the person you'll become.

As I mentioned, I never wanted to be an entrepreneur—it wasn't a vocation, an option, or even a goal I aspired to.

I grew up with my mother, a single parent who worked tirelessly to raise us, provide our education, and maintain a stable home. All three of us children admired her courage, determination, and spirit of sacrifice.

I remember thinking that if I could become half the woman she was, I would consider myself accomplished.

After turning 30, she returned to university, driven by her lifelong desire to learn and to make up for missed educational opportunities in her youth. Though her master's degree in education didn't advance her career, she demonstrated that one could simultaneously work, raise children, and pursue higher education. Her career transitions, particularly her final change, made for personal fulfillment, taught us that work could be a source of pleasure, joy, and satisfaction. For these lessons, I'm deeply grateful. My mother remains my greatest source of inspiration.

Yet despite her example, my siblings and I grew up in an environment where, although our needs were met, we were conditioned to avoid taking too many risks.

The Journey I Expected to Take

I always wanted to be a lawyer. Once, in kindergarten, when asked about my parents' jobs—before their separation—I didn't know what to say. So, I asked them. My father explained he was a lawyer and my mother a legal assistant. I memorised these words to repeat at school, though neither my classmates nor I understood what they meant. A little girl insisted it couldn't be true. When I asked why, she replied that a lawyer was a fruit… "Isn't your father a fruit?" (In French, the word "avocat" means both "avocado" and "lawyer")

No, indeed, my father was not a fruit!

Confused and frustrated, I went back to my parents and told them the story, admitting I didn't really understand what they did for a living.

They took the time to explain. My father told me that a lawyer's job was to defend people who couldn't defend themselves, keep them out of jail, and give them a voice. That was all I needed—at four years old, I knew I wanted to be a lawyer like my dad.

The fact that my mother worked in the same legal environment, though not with him, gave me a sense of natural progression. It felt like I had found my path.

Years later, in high school, I discovered philosophy. As someone who loved books, poems, and words, I was captivated by the reflection it required. I became fascinated by authors like Sartre and his companion Simone de Beauvoir, as well as Nietzsche and Descartes. On the eve of my A-level, I told my mother I wanted to study philosophy instead of law.

She responded pragmatically: "Philosophy isn't a profession. Go to law school—you'll have your whole life to philosophise afterwards."

This seemed non-negotiable and not very reassuring for career guidance, so I chose law, anyway, we're all lawyers in my family...

I passed my baccalaureate and enrolled in law school. My parents were thrilled, and I was motivated to learn how to defend people who needed a voice.

I approached my studies seriously and diligently, while also working to maintain financial independence. But in my second year, I began having moral dilemmas. Though I was passionate about law, major criminal trials were making headlines. When the DUTROUX case exploded in France and Belgium, heated discussions arose at the university: How do you defend a pedophile?

While everyone deserves the right to defence—a sacred principle—I questioned whether this was the context in which I wanted to practice and make my voice heard. My love for travel led me to explore other opportunities, which resonated more deeply. I decided to work for international organisations, focusing on development, access to education, school building, and defending people's right to self-determination.

I'm specialising, and becoming an attorney is slowly disappearing from the scope, preferring negotiation and alternative dispute resolution.

Life's Pivotal Moments Rarely Arrive On Schedule— Uncertainty Is Simply Part Of The Journey

I met the man who would become my husband. He was living with his parents while recovering from a motorcycle accident in California, where a hit-and-run driver had left him unconscious on the road.

At the time we met, he was unemployed and in rehabilitation. I was a student, supporting myself by tutoring children and living independently in a small apartment near the university. My dream was simple: to return to London, where I had spent a wonderful year working and learning English.

Neither of us was looking for a relationship—he planned to return to work in the States, and I was set on London. We thought we'd only be here in Paris for a year. Life had other plans.

His parents, uncomfortable with him living at home, gave him an ultimatum six months into our relationship: find a job or leave the apartment. Despite finding a job, they gave him a few months to leave the place. That's how we ended up falling deeply in love, living together, followed by an equally unplanned marriage.

We were working and living in Paris at the time, but wanted to move abroad again, as we had both planned before meeting each other.

Life's Lessons Unfold When Plans Falter, Sparking Meaningful Change

All my attempts to find a job abroad failed.

Watching my dreams slip away left me distraught.

I began asking myself fundamental questions: *What are my skills? What do I want to do? What drives me? How could I make a meaningful contribution?*

I started filling notebooks with ideas and thoughts. Initially, it was unstructured—just capturing ideas and seeing where they would lead.

Over time, I discovered a focus that aligned with my interests and expertise: helping aspiring entrepreneurs.

I delved deeper into this area and encountered a striking statistic—over 80% of startups fail within their first three years. This number shocked me. I realised that if I could create a support toolkit, I might help business owners overcome these challenges. After all, entrepreneurs aren't lacking intelligence; they face specific challenges and need specific solutions. Why not create a toolkit to highlight potential pitfalls and guide them in the right direction?

This insight led me to develop my 8-step method, building upon and expanding the traditional business plan approach.

Turning Vision Into Value

When I started my business, several crucial insights emerged.

I tested my idea for a year while keeping my day job, wanting to validate whether people would actually pay for my offering. The response was encouraging, I gained a steady stream of clients who compensated me through alternative means, like sports lessons for my daughter or golf lessons for my husband. Then one day, a client asked about my fee—something I hadn't even considered.

I requested a day to think about pricing, and when I quoted what was honestly an arbitrary figure, the client responded, "That's far too low for what you're offering. You should charge more for your next client."

I had underpriced because I thought I was simply providing entrepreneurs with a toolkit, not realising I was offering a comprehensive support service.

Through this experience, I discovered two key insights:

- The strength of entrepreneurs' visions and convictions
- The fact that, beyond a toolkit, entrepreneurs need someone to support them, especially when they're starting and more generally in times of doubt.

I didn't realise then that what I was doing was coaching and consulting entrepreneurs in developing their projects. I simply knew I wanted to help people bring their projects to life. There was something beautiful about helping others make their dreams a reality.

The journey was inspiring and educational. Some lessons can't be explained—they must be experienced to be understood.

The entrepreneurial path isn't easy. You must constantly make decisions and own their consequences, even those you couldn't have anticipated. Nothing is entirely predictable!

The Mindset

Through working with entrepreneurs and becoming one myself, I've come to realise the importance of resilience. Starting involves a profound phase of change.

Being an entrepreneur isn't easy—you must face uncertainty, never knowing for certain whether your venture will succeed.

It's true that you don't know, or at least you can't be sure, but as we've seen, it's like life: nothing is written and nothing is linear. On the other hand, it's not easy to undertake and try to have a better life, and in the other direction, it works too; it's not easy to have a job you don't like and live a life you don't like either.

This is where transformation begins: change only happens when the pain of staying the same exceeds the pain of changing.

Indeed, if the pain isn't greater than the fear of change, there's no reason to leave our comfort zone. Why complicate life?

The hardest part is that initial leap into the unknown. I think that once you realise that it can be done, you're less afraid. That's when the mindset kicks in.

You're Not Born an Entrepreneur, You Become One

Each day, you grow more accustomed to finding solutions despite the discomfort of change. Eventually, this discomfort becomes familiar—even energising—turning into your natural territory.

That's why I compare the entrepreneurial mindset to two distinct paths:

- **Sportsmen and women:** Just as race car drivers must focus on where they want to go rather than the obstacles they want to avoid, entrepreneurs need to move forward with unwavering conviction. An entrepreneur's vision acts as their compass. That's what vision is for the entrepreneur: he can't afford to fixate on problems but must concentrate on their direction and goals. Then all that remains is to be consistent, and that requires discipline, just like an athlete.

- **Artists:** An entrepreneur, like an artist, must remain true to their authentic self. I believe that every artist is an entrepreneur who ignores himself, and every entrepreneur is an artist who ignores himself. Both face moments of creation where they must materialise their vision, whether as a product, service, or company. When presenting their work to the world, feedback can be intensely positive or negative. That's why maintaining perspective is crucial: remember that criticism of the creation isn't criticism of the creator— sometimes, a proposal simply hasn't found its audience yet.

Entrepreneurship Is Mastered Through Failures and Moments of Doubt

When you're an entrepreneur, you must deconstruct what you've learned to be able to move forward, because we're conditioned and we're not taught to be good at everything you need to be an entrepreneur (finance, law, HR, marketing, etc.).

Entrepreneurship is about working as part of a group so that you can share and grow with others.

I draw a lot of parallels between life and entrepreneurship because it seems to me that entrepreneurship is a metaphor for life. From this angle, it allows us to look at it differently, objectively and benevolently, and it helps us to see this freedom as an adventure rather than as a risk so enormous that the fear becomes insurmountable.

This perspective makes entrepreneurship less daunting and may inspire people to act and share their vision with the world—something I deeply believe we need.

When you're doing something you love, it doesn't feel like work. However, this can be dangerous—you might find yourself working around the clock without realising how exhausted you've become.

Motivation is the driving force behind your business—it's what separates those who succeed from those who don't. Your motivation, regardless of its source, lies at the heart of your project. It gives you the strength to persevere and reinvent yourself when needed.

Remember one thing: The most important thing is not the first gain, but the following ones.

Today, I'm changing lives and making an impact in my own way.

If there's one message I'd like to share here, it's this: take action. Start with something small—declare yourself an author on LinkedIn when you begin writing a book, or talk openly about that side business you started two years ago. The key is to start expressing your authentic voice and to play your own music without fear.

Draw inspiration from others and let your journey inspire those around you!

Dr. Gina Kuhn-Robatin

Founder and CEO of Dr. Gina's Transformation Academy, LLC

www.linkedin.com/in/dr-gina-kuhn-robatin
https://www.facebook.com/gina.kuhnrobatin
https://drginasacademy.com/

A dynamic force of inspiration, Dr. Gina Kuhn-Robatin is a multi-passion entrepreneur, award-winning speaker and singer with over 30 years in business. Her journey began helping her father in his trophy shop and blossomed into a legacy of leadership, innovation, and heart-led hustle. From selling products at fairs to touring the nation in a bus with her singing family, she's mastered the art of balancing business with purpose. After surviving a stroke and redefining her path, she launched her signature empowerment program, D.R.E.A.M. In Motion, helping women ignite their passion, align their priorities, and live fulfilled lives. Known for her sparkle, authenticity, unstoppable energy, she empowers professional women to rise above burnout and walk boldly in their calling. With a deep faith, fierce love for her family, and a mission to uplift others, she proves that resilience, reinvention, and authenticity are the true keys to success.

Born to Build: A Legacy of Entrepreneurship

By Dr. Gina Kuhn-Robatin

Entrepreneurship isn't just something I do, it's in my blood. It's the rhythm of my life, the legacy passed down through generations, and the foundation upon which I've built my success. As I celebrate 30 years in business, I reflect on the incredible journey that has shaped me into the entrepreneur I am today.

The Roots of Entrepreneurship

From the earliest days of my childhood, business wasn't just something we did, it was who we were. My first memories of work weren't in a traditional office or behind a desk; they were in my father's trophy business, where I helped him craft awards that symbolize excellence. I was fascinated by the precision, care, and attention to detail he put into creating custom pieces for his customers. The joy on the customers' faces when they saw their finished product was astounding. My little hands would spend many nights after school building trophies for my dad. Most nights, my grandmother would join me in my efforts. She was always there to help out. Simply working alongside her and listening to her stories made building trophies even more meaningful. We would talk about who we thought might be receiving them and imagine how they would feel. Sometimes, we would build trophies as high as 5 feet. They were usually made for the raceway. One time a year, we would have "Kuhn's Trophy Night" at the raceway, and I would have the honor of handing them out as the trophy girl. I would look forward to meeting the winners. That was truly a highlight of my childhood. I once had a friend whose father won the championship. I'll never forget seeing him receive that huge trophy.

My father wasn't just a businessman; he was a visionary. His entrepreneurial spirit extended far beyond trophies, and soon, our family was immersed in both the advertising and the sporting goods industry. This new adventure meant long hours, dedication, and a lifestyle that revolved around business. I remember traveling across Pennsylvania, helping Dad set up equipment at wrestling tournaments, ensuring that athletes could have the best equipment. I witnessed firsthand what it took to run a business on the move. My dad was relentless in his pursuit of success, and in him, I saw the qualities that would later define my own entrepreneurial journey: grit, determination, and an unwavering commitment to excellence.

The Leap into the Fair and Entertainment Industry

Entrepreneurship wasn't just my father's pursuit; it became a family affair. As I grew older and built a life of my own, my husband and I found ourselves deeply intertwined with my parents' next adventure, the Fair and Entertainment industry. This industry was a whirlwind of energy, excitement, and unpredictability. We set up at fairs, festivals, and large events, bringing food, products, and experience to people who were out to enjoy themselves.

The fair world was unlike anything else. It required an understanding of consumer behavior, the ability to market effectively in short bursts, and the flexibility to adapt to different crowds and environments. There was a thrill in watching people light up when they found something they loved at our stand. Every fair, every event was a new opportunity to connect, sell, and grow.

Through these experiences, I honed my skills in business strategy, customer engagement, and the art of creating an unforgettable experience. I learned how to navigate challenges, from unpredictable weather to fluctuating crowd sizes, and how to turn obstacles into opportunities. The fair and entertainment industry cemented my ability to think on my feet, embrace change, and create success in the most dynamic of environments.

A Family on the Road

From the fair and entertainment industry, our family found ourselves drawn into another vibrant, fast-paced world, selling hair products across the country. This wasn't your typical business operation. We weren't sitting behind desks or working in a single location. Instead, we packed up, hit the road, and traveled from state to state, setting up booths, engaging with customers, and learning the art of sales in its most dynamic form.

This chapter of my journey was more than just business; it was about adaptability, resilience, and family adventure. My children grew up both watching and helping their parents and grandparents work hard. They not only saw it, but they were able to work alongside us. My boys experienced firsthand that success wasn't handed to us; it was earned through strategic decisions, commitment, and hard work.

Traveling the country selling hair products taught me the importance of customer service, resilience, and the ability to pivot. Every new location meant different people, different needs, and different challenges. The one thing that remained constant was our ability to connect with people, understand their needs, and provide value. These lessons would serve me well as I branched out into my own entrepreneurial endeavors.

Carrying The Legacy Forward

Growing up, all I knew was entrepreneurship. It was the language we spoke at the dinner table, the lifestyle we lived, and the mindset that shaped every decision. It was never about waiting for opportunities, it was about creating them.

When it came time for me to step fully into my own as an entrepreneur, I knew I wanted to carry forward the legacy my family had built while also carving out my own path. Over the years, I have owned multiple businesses across different industries, each one an extension of my passion, skills, purpose, and vision.

From my work as a professional singer, where we built a brand around inspiration, faith, motivation, and empowerment, to my real estate investments, where we have created opportunities for families to live in beautiful spaces. Every business has been an expression of who I am. My career as a medical massage therapist allowed me to impact lives both mentally and physically, while my role as a public speaker, life coach, and course creator has allowed me to empower women to live with confidence, balance, and fulfillment. Living with purpose.

Entrepreneurship, for me, has never been just about one thing. It's been about using my skills, experience, passion, and purpose to create businesses that serve and inspire others. It has been about resilience, adaptability, and the willingness to step into the unknown with faith and determination.

30 Years of Entrepreneurship and Beyond

This year marks 30 years since I first stepped into the world of business on my own. It's a milestone that fills me with immense gratitude and pride. I have navigated challenges, embraced growth, and continued to evolve as an entrepreneur. I have built businesses that not only provide for my family but also empower others to pursue their dreams.

Through it all, one thing has remained constant: my commitment to living authentically and helping others do the same. Whether through my D.R.E.A.M. In Motion program and my work as a professional woman, my mission is clear: to inspire others to create lives of purpose, balance, joy, and fulfillment.

Looking back, I see the little girl in her father's trophy shop, watching, learning, dreaming, and wanting to win my own trophy someday. I see the young woman traveling the country selling, adapting, and growing. Today, I see that same woman as strong, seasoned, and deeply committed to empowering others through the entrepreneurial legacy that has shaped my life.

As I step into the next chapter of my journey, I do so with excitement, confidence, and the unwavering belief that the best is yet to come. Because entrepreneurship isn't just what I do, it's who I am!

Corrie Gallien

Gallien Law
Attorney

https://www.linkedin.com/in/corriegallien/
https://www.facebook.com/corriegallien1/
https://www.instagram.com/corriegallien
https://gallienlaw.com/

Corrie R. Gallien, Esq., is a deaf attorney, disability advocate, and founder of Gallien Law, where she focuses on personal injury, appellate practice, and legal research and writing support for fellow attorneys. A proud Louisiana native and first-generation college graduate, she earned her Juris Doctor from LSU's Paul M. Hebert Law Center in 2011 and has over a decade of legal experience in both litigation and advocacy.

Corrie's work is rooted in compassion, strategy, and empowerment—values shaped by her personal journey through disability and domestic abuse. She brings her voice to multiple arenas—as a juvenile public defender, community leader, and a rising figure in writing and public speaking. Her upcoming book, "Personal Injury: The Economic Impact of Domestic Abuse," explores the financial toll of abuse and the legal tools available to survivors.

Entrepreneurship:
The Path I Never Thought I'd Take

By Corrie Gallien

I. This Wasn't the Plan

I have been an attorney for over thirteen years. Throughout my legal career, I have had the opportunity to represent countless individuals with a variety of legal issues at the district and appellate levels. I have handled cases in state and federal courts. Despite my legal accomplishments and client success stories, I often felt inadequate.

Although most attorneys exude confidence, leadership, and charisma, I typically felt comfortable playing a background role in my professional career. I looked to other attorneys for guidance and job opportunities. Throughout my legal career, I've held numerous roles: clerk for judges, associate attorney, contract attorney, of counsel, and more.

Had you asked me right out of law school whether I would ever 'hang my own shingle,' I would have responded with a resounding no.

II. Why I Didn't Think Entrepreneurship Was for Me

Looking back on things, I had a lofty idea of what it meant to be an entrepreneur. You had to be bold, extroverted, and popular—and I didn't see myself as any of these.

Beyond these perceptions, I had two very personal reasons why I counted myself out of entrepreneurship.

"Deafness Held Me Back"

First, I am profoundly deaf. My deafness is genetic; I've been hard of hearing since birth. As I got older, it progressively worsened. By the time I reached college, I couldn't hear anything the professors were saying in lecture halls.

Deafness is an invisible disability that affects your ability to comprehend sound. As a child, I constantly feared being perceived as unintelligent or less than due to my disability. I worked hard to mask it. I relied on context clues, facial expressions, lip reading, and multitasking to fill in the gaps between what I could hear and what was actually being said. It was not perfect, but many people were unaware that I was deaf.

Masking my deafness was exhausting. It made me worried that people would question my abilities as an attorney. Rather than ask people to repeat themselves, I often pretended to understand. I knew people sometimes become frustrated when asked to repeat things, and as a recovering people pleaser, speaking up felt too hard.

However, pretending to understand often led to the very thing I feared: appearing unintelligent. Masking became a daily emotional rollercoaster—exhausting and unsustainable. I ended most days frustrated, anxious, and overwhelmed.

I didn't just mask my disability—I also hid in the background because of it. I gravitated toward research and writing rather than oral advocacy. Being in court was completely overwhelming for me as a deaf attorney. Deafness became one of the biggest hurdles I faced on the path to entrepreneurship.

In 2019, I received cochlear implants, which have artificially restored my hearing. My hearing in quiet environments is now in the normal range. Still, the technology isn't perfect. I must keep my batteries charged and monitor my equipment regularly. The surgery removed any remaining natural hearing I had, so when I remove my processor, I am completely deaf. Despite the drawbacks, my implants have helped me better navigate the courtrooms and my daily life.

"Abuse Made Me Shrink"

Another reason I shied away from entrepreneurship was that I went through an abusive marriage that wrecked my confidence. Abuse is a form of control that makes you believe you need the other person to survive—that you are not good enough on your own. I shrunk under the emotional abuse throughout my marriage. After I courageously left, it culminated in a final experience that was deeply abusive.

Recovering from the abuse was a challenge. To combat the burnout, I had to focus on myself and my family. I temporarily stepped away from my career as an attorney. Entrepreneurship was completely off my radar. I have gone through years of therapy and have come out stronger, healed, and happy.

What happened at the end of my marriage was not just painful—it was violating and life-altering. I share more about that experience and its impact in my book, *Personal Injury: The Economic Impact of Abusive Relationships*, where I give voice to the silence I once lived with. In it, I reflect on the emotional and financial cost of abuse, how I began the journey back to myself, and how other survivors can, too.

III. The Shift – "The Turning Point I Didn't See Coming"

I began to consider entrepreneurship when I met a colleague who had her own law firm and was interested in forming a partnership with me. Our partnership lasted only two years, and when I walked away, I left thousands of earned dollars on the table—losses I'm still trying to recover from. Where leaving my abusive relationship was my personal rock bottom, leaving my partnership was my professional rock bottom.

During our time together, my partner controlled all the firm's finances. I didn't have access to the books or a clear picture of where the money was going. That imbalance of control mirrored past relationships where I had silenced my voice or deferred my power—and it left me unprepared for what true entrepreneurship would require.

Although our partnership was short-lived and rocky, it showed me that entrepreneurship was possible. I realized that I could not come into another attorney's firm and expect them to work like me, think like me, or do business like me.

I could not fix systems I thought were broken if I didn't create or own those systems.

After I made the decision to leave my partnership in 2024, I quickly made the decision to found my own firm, Gallien Law, where I focus on personal injury, appellate law, and legal research and writing.

IV. The Leap – "Doing It Afraid"

Taking the leap into entrepreneurship was—and still is—scary. It shook me up and instilled a deep sense of purpose. Although I didn't have a clear roadmap before getting started, I did what I do best: I researched how to start a business and a law firm. I also participated in programs, joined organizations, and attended classes that helped me develop entrepreneurial skills.

The biggest internal challenge I've faced is imposter syndrome. Whether it stems from a lifetime of shrinking due to deafness or the confidence erosion caused by my abusive marriage, I battled a quiet but persistent feeling that I didn't belong in the entrepreneurial world.

Externally, the biggest hurdle has been limited financial resources. My finances and credit profile were decimated by my divorce. I poured every dollar I had into creating Gallien Law, without a large book of business or financial safety net.

As a single mother of four girls, I often questioned whether I could maintain our lifestyle or even keep up with the basics. Downsizing my car or home during this time wasn't an option due to my damaged credit.

The moment I almost threw in the towel was when I was offered a job that came with a six-figure salary—more than enough to meet my family's needs—but came with a full-time, exclusive commitment. Accepting that offer would have required me to close the doors of Gallien Law. I almost took it. I almost said yes.

V. The Growth – "Building What I Didn't Know I Needed"

Accepting the job offer was tempting, but I knew Gallien Law wasn't birthed by accident. Although I didn't originally believe entrepreneurship was for me, I knew I shouldn't give up on it so easily.

While I haven't yet matched the income from that job opportunity, entrepreneurship has given me the flexibility I need—and the chance to build something on my own terms. It hasn't been a full year since I opened the doors of Gallien Law, so I welcome the opportunity to exceed that benchmark. I have a passion for what I do, and I do it well. As a result, my firm and I are gaining the visibility we need to succeed.

The only way I could work at my ideal firm was by creating it myself.

Personal injury representation is a highly saturated area of law, yet I know I will be successful. Where I plant my seeds and water them, I will harvest fruit. Since founding Gallien Law, I have successfully resolved multiple clients' personal injury cases. Getting my clients the compensation that they deserve is a huge win—for them, and for me.

Appellate law is a nuanced and overlooked area, largely due to the high cost of appealing an unfavorable ruling. The cost barrier has made it my slowest-growing practice area. Still, I am not discouraged by the pace. I continue to position myself as an authority in appellate law and trust that the investments I'm making now will pay off in the long run.

Additionally, my legal collaborations have been growing steadily. Satisfied attorneys have recommended me to colleagues, which has led to opportunities to support Louisiana lawyers with legal research and writing across a wide variety of cases.

My entrepreneurial journey with Gallien Law is still unfolding. I hope to scale my firm across Louisiana in all three practice areas. For personal injury victims and individuals seeking appeals, my goal is to provide accessible care, clear guidance, and unwavering dedication to their recovery and legal relief. I also strive to become a trusted resource for overworked attorneys seeking high-quality legal research and writing—helping them lighten their load and avoid the burnout I once experienced.

VI. The Reflection – "This Path Chose Me Too"

One of the most powerful parts of this journey has been learning to stop hiding. I no longer mask my disability or pretend it doesn't exist. I now embrace it fully, and I've become a proud advocate for the disability community. Sharing my experience publicly has allowed me to connect with others, break down stereotypes, and show that leadership comes in many forms. My journey has taught me that my voice matters—not despite my deafness, but, in part, because of it.

I have also learned to stop shrinking myself and hiding in the background. I have so much to offer the legal community—and the world. Reclaiming my personal and professional independence has been nothing short of liberating. Not only do I give myself permission to be seen and heard, but I also encourage you to do the same.

As I look back on how far I have come on this entrepreneurial journey, I am grateful for how it has reshaped my life. It has encouraged me to put myself out there and strengthen my personal and professional brand.

Entrepreneurship has also deepened my community involvement. I participate in leadership programs and legal workshops to help the community. I also attend community expos to inform the public about Gallien Law and the services I offer.

I've come to understand that I didn't just accept this path—it chose me. While I may not be naturally extroverted, I continue to strengthen my confidence, communication, and leadership skills. Contrary to what many believe, entrepreneurship isn't meant to be a lonely journey. Just as it takes a village to raise a child, it takes a community to support a business.

If you are unsure of whether entrepreneurship is right for you, I want you to know this: It can exceed your wildest imagination. You don't have to be born with every tool and skill. If you're willing to do the work and build the right connections, your business—and your confidence—will thrive.

VII. Closing Words – "Keep Walking"

Entrepreneurship is not the path of least resistance. You will meet many obstacles on this journey, but I invite you to consider the path you never imagined for yourself. You are capable. You are worthy. You are enough.

Every day I live to reassure the deaf child who hid in the shadows that she is out here living a dream she never thought possible.

"What I once feared became the freedom I never knew I needed. I'm still building, but now—I walk boldly."

You, too, can have this freedom that comes with entrepreneurship. My two pieces of advice: ignore the doubt and start now.

JOIN THE MOVEMENT!
#BAUW

Becoming An Unstoppable Woman
With She Rises Studios

She Rises Studios was founded by Hanna Olivas and Adriana Luna Carlos, the mother-daughter duo, in mid-2020 as they saw a need to help empower women worldwide. They are the podcast hosts of the *She Rises Studios Podcast* and Amazon best-selling authors and motivational speakers who travel the world. Hanna and Adriana are the movement creators of #BAUW - Becoming An Unstoppable Woman: The movement has been created to universally impact women of all ages, at whatever stage of life, to overcome insecurities, and adversities, and develop an unstoppable mindset. She Rises Studios educates, celebrates, and empowers women globally.

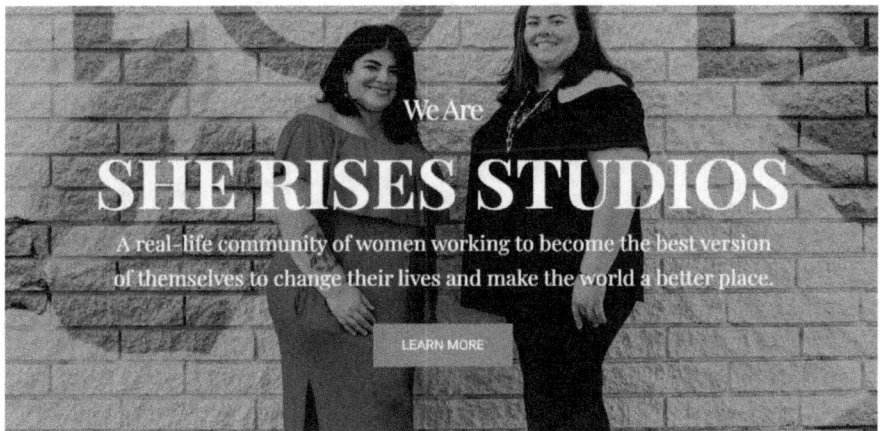

Looking to Join Us in our Next Anthology or Publish YOUR Own?

She Rises Studios Publishing offers full-service publishing, marketing, book tour, and campaign services. For more information, contact info@sherisesstudios.com

We are always looking for women who want to share their stories and expertise and feature their businesses on our podcasts, in our books, and in our magazines.

SEE WHAT WE DO

OUR PODCAST   **OUR BOOKS**   **OUR SERVICES**

Be featured in the Becoming An Unstoppable Woman magazine, published in 13 countries and sold in all major retailers. Get the visibility you need to LEVEL UP in your business!

Have your own TV show streamed across major platforms like Roku TV, Amazon Fire Stick, Apple TV and more!

Learn to leverage your expertise. Build your online presence and grow your audience with FENIX TV.
https://fenixtv.sherisesstudios.com/

Visit www.SheRisesStudios.com to see how YOU can join the #BAUW movement and help your community to achieve the UNSTOPPABLE mindset.

Have you checked out the *She Rises Studios Podcast?*

Find us on all MAJOR platforms: Spotify, IHeartRadio, Apple Podcasts, Google Podcasts, etc.

Looking to become a sponsor or build a partnership?

Email us at info@sherisesstudios.com

www.ingramcontent.com/pod-product-compliance
Lightning Source LLC
Chambersburg PA
CBHW071318120626
46546CB00002B/368